Praise for *Tools for Teaching Conceptual Understanding, Secondary*

"Stern, Ferraro, and Mohnkern tear down the false dichotomy of traditional versus innovative education and provides the clarion call and practical tool kit for developing creativity by building and applying knowledge through Concept-Based learning. Every practitioner needs this book to juxtapose what worked well in the 20th century with what is essential in the 21st century and beyond."

—*Michael McDowell*
Superintendent
Ross School District, Ross, CA

"If you are ready to have students really learn, get ready to be amazed. Here is the complete guide to creating your very own Concept-Based classroom. I have never read a book filled with so many great ideas that can be used in any classroom."

—*Amanda McKee*
Secondary Mathematics Instructor
Johnsonville High School, SC

"This book is as essential to a teacher utilizing Concept-Based teaching as the approach of Concept-Based learning is essential to teaching."

—*Ayo Magwood*
Social Studies Teacher
Maret Private School, Washington, DC

"I can't recommend this book enough! Exceptionally practical pedagogical techniques that are steeped in bags of authentic research. Addressing how children learn, how teachers can plan lessons within a conceptual framework, specific and useful differentiation techniques and feedback methods—so many meaningful and highly effective ways to move learners forward, preparing them for the future in a meaningful way."

—*Julia Briggs*
Certified Concept-Based trainer, IB Science Teacher and Chemistry Coordinator
Colegio Anglo-Colombiano, Bogotá, Colombia

D1710053

"This book addresses the need for students to learn critical dispositions and skills which go beyond traditional discipline knowledge and are essential for student success as innovators in the 21st century."

—*Brenda Booth*
Instructional Coach
Burlington-Edison School District, Burlington, WA

"While most good educators recognize the incredible value of teaching conceptually, it is challenging. Julie Stern, Krista Ferraro and Juliet Mohnkern have created accessible, practical baby steps for every teacher to use."

—*Dr. Vincent Chan*
Principal
Fairview International School, Kuala Lumpur, Malaysia

"The authors of *Tools for Teaching Conceptual Understanding* have crafted an incredible resource for teachers in secondary education. This book provides a strong rationale on the importance of Concept-Based Curriculum development in the classroom for the 21st century. The book delivers a framework on how to build a Concept-Based classroom from the ground up, offering practical, easy-to-apply tools and techniques that will allow teachers to redesign their curriculum in a rigorous way, while providing a classroom environment of deep learning. From developing great lesson plans to on-point assessments that target conceptual understanding, this book is an incredible resource for classroom teachers".

—*Maria Cardona*
Middle School Science IB Instructor
Corbett Preparatory School of IDS

"Perhaps the most significant question every educationist asks today is how to meet the needs of all learners in a classroom. Conceptual learning teaches for deep understanding and enables students to find patterns and make connections, thus providing intellectual dignity. In the section on differentiation, there are clear action steps with examples as support for reaching out to all students. A must-read for all who are committed to Concept-Based teaching and instruction!"

—*Mona Seervai*
Former Principal, Bombay International School
IB Workshop Leader and Consultant, Certified Concept-Based Trainer

"Stern, Ferraro, and Mohnkern have truly 'drilled down' the Concept-Based framework, providing an understandable guide for teaching and assessing conceptual understanding. This book should be a 'go to' resource for every teacher!"

—*Susanne Long*
Director of Curriculum, Research, and Development Services
Onslow County School System, Jacksonville, NC

"Stern, Ferraro and Mohnkern's method provides a lucid framework to deepen conceptual understanding. Building upon the foundation laid by Erickson and Lanning, this approach provides tangible strategies for classroom teachers to nurture deeper learning."

—*Richard Healy*
Deputy Head of Secondary School
Colegio Anglo Colombiano, Bogotá, Colombia

"As the product, and facilitator, of a topic-based, coverage-centered education for some four decades, discovering the value of a Concept-Based approach to teaching and learning has caused a paradigmatic shift both in my classroom and in my own intellectual journey. Julie Stern, Krista Ferraro and Juliet Mohnkern´s book builds upon the best of recent educational theory and research to guide teachers on how to transform our students from fact-collectors into conceptual experts as they discover and transfer their understandings of the world around them, and ultimately, seek to solve real-world challenges."

—*Neville Kirton*
Head of Humanities Department
Colegio Anglo Colombiano, Bogotá, Colombia

"*Tools for Teaching Conceptual Understanding* is filled with assessments and ideas for teaching students to think conceptually in the classroom. Teachers can learn tools for developing student thinking and how to continually assess for conceptual *understanding* as learning happens. I recommend this book for anyone who is looking to develop lessons and assessments to support deep, conceptual thinking in their classroom."

—*Amy Reisner*
Assistant Principal, District Concept-Based Trainer
Bay View Elementary, Burlington, WA

Concept-Based Curriculum and Instruction— Series List

Concept-Based Curriculum and Instruction for the Thinking Classroom, 2nd edition—H. Lynn Erickson, Lois A. Lanning, and Rachel French

This resource offers a complete guide to designing curriculum and instruction that moves teaching and learning beyond lower level facts and skills to deep conceptual understanding.

Stirring the Heart, Head, and Soul: Redefining Curriculum, Instruction, and Concept-Based Learning, 3rd edition—H. Lynn Erickson

This book examines the current state of curriculum and instruction and proposes a curricular plan for achieving higher standards without sacrificing intellectual integrity.

Facilitator's Guide to Stirring the Heart, Head, and Soul: Redefining Curriculum, Instruction, and Concept-Based Learning, 3rd edition—H. Lynn Erickson

This guide gives staff developers and workshop leaders the tools to help teachers gain a clear understanding of how to use Concept-Based Instruction to deepen students' understandings and inspire a genuine love of learning.

Transitioning to Concept-Based Curriculum and Instruction: How to Bring Content and Process Together—H. Lynn Erickson and Lois A. Lanning

In this book, teachers will learn how to use the Structure of Process and Structure of Knowledge in designing Concept-Based Curriculum and units. Leaders and coaches will find advice for staff development.

Designing a Concept-Based Curriculum for English Language Arts: Meeting the Common Core With Intellectual Integrity, K-12—Lois A. Lanning

All of the recent research about learning, as well as current standards, mark a shift toward conceptual understanding of complex processes. In this "how-to" book, Lois A. Lanning introduces the Structure of Process as a tool to aid English language arts teachers (and teachers of other process-driven disciplines) in designing high quality Concept-Based units for the classroom.

Concept-Based Mathematics: Teaching for Deep Understanding in Secondary Classrooms—Jennie Wathall

When you teach concepts rather than rote processes, students see math's essential elegance, as well as its practicality—and discover their own natural mathematical abilities. This book is a road map to retooling how you teach math in a deep, clear, and meaningful way—through a conceptual lens—helping students achieve higher order thinking skills.

Tools for Teaching Conceptual Understanding, Elementary: Designing Lessons and Assessments for Deep Learning—Julie Stern, Nathalie Lauriault, and Krista Ferraro

This guide provides instructional strategies for use in the elementary classroom. Teachers will learn how to teach metacognitive skills to young students and design lessons for conceptual understanding.

Tools for Teaching Conceptual Understanding, Secondary: Designing Lessons and Assessments for Deep Learning—Julie Stern, Krista Ferraro, and Juliet Mohnkern

This guide provides instructional strategies for use in the secondary classroom. Teachers will learn how to introduce secondary students to conceptual thinking and design lessons across disciplines for conceptual understanding.

Tools for Teaching Conceptual Understanding, Secondary

For Dr. H. Lynn Erickson—may your legacy stir the heads, hearts, and souls of generations to come.

Tools for Teaching Conceptual Understanding, Secondary

Designing Lessons and Assessments for Deep Learning

Julie Stern

Krista Ferraro

Juliet Mohnkern

Foreword by H. Lynn Erickson and Lois A. Lanning

CORWIN
A SAGE Publishing Company

FOR INFORMATION:

Corwin

A SAGE Company

2455 Teller Road

Thousand Oaks, California 91320

(800) 233-9936

www.corwin.com

SAGE Publications Ltd.

1 Oliver's Yard

55 City Road

London EC1Y 1SP

United Kingdom

SAGE Publications India Pvt. Ltd.

B 1/I 1 Mohan Cooperative Industrial Area

Mathura Road, New Delhi 110 044

India

SAGE Publications Asia-Pacific Pte. Ltd.

3 Church Street

#10-04 Samsung Hub

Singapore 049483

Acquisitions Editor: Ariel Bartlett

Senior Associate Editor: Desirée A. Bartlett

Editorial Assistant: Kaitlyn Irwin

Production Editor: Amy Schroller

Copy Editor: Tina Hardy

Typesetter: Hurix Systems Pvt. Ltd.

Proofreader: Jeff Bryant

Indexer: Rick Hurd

Cover Designer: Scott Van Atta

Marketing Manager: Jill Margulies

Printed in the United States of America

ISBN 978-1-5063-5570-2

This book is printed on acid-free paper.

17 18 19 20 21 10 9 8 7 6 5 4 3 2 1

Contents

Foreword

What does a thinking student look like? In this book, Julie Stern, Krista Ferraro, and Juliet Mohnkern share their vision of thinking students and how teachers make that vision a reality.

The attributes of a thinking student, which this book describes, bring to mind the main character of the highly popular *Maisie Dobbs* mystery series. In the series, writer Jacqueline Winspear chronicles the lives of several characters and stories within stories across time. Maisie Dobbs, the main character, is a psychologist and investigator. She is fascinating on many levels, but one of the traits that stands out is her inquiry work that just won't let her go. She becomes so immersed in each case that she struggles to break away. Maisie tackles investigations searching for answers. One of her trusty tools is a "case map" that she creates using colored crayons and pencils to graphically capture relationships and patterns among emerging clues and to record questions that cause reflection and further digging. Although the Maisie Dobbs stories begin in the early 1900s, her patience, curiosity, perseverance, and mindfulness are characteristics that are just as prized and relevant today.

People often lament, "Education has not changed in 50 years, except we are trying to cover more faster, using technology to speed the process." As educators for over four decades, we understand the expression of concern, because teaching and learning still appear to be driven more by coverage of content, drill on skills, and an increase in test scores. But this book, *Tools for Teaching Conceptual Understanding, Secondary: Designing Lessons and Assessments for Deep Learning*—the latest contribution to the collection of books on Concept-Based Curriculum and Instruction—illustrates the shift that is taking place in rethinking curriculum design, teaching, and learning around the world.

What *has* changed over the past 50 years is our deeper understanding of how knowledge and processes are structured, the importance of conceptual transfer, how the brain works, how to differentiate instruction for varied learners, and effective versus ineffective pedagogical methods. The task now is to help all teachers internalize these findings and move them into classroom practice, which is exactly what this book does.

Tools for Teaching Conceptual Understanding, Secondary: Designing Lessons and Assessments for Deep Learning provides a sound overview of Concept-Based Curriculum and

Instruction and then speaks directly to teaching and learning in thinking classrooms. The book honors the work of educational leaders, such as Richard Paul and Linda Elder, Ron Ritchhart, and Carol Dweck, and offers a valuable toolbox of strategies for helping students metacognitively analyze their own thought processes. Teachers will especially appreciate the ideas that focus on student intellectual growth. "Thinking" has long been a goal of instruction, but there was little support, until more recently, for exactly *how* to do this without making "thinking" a stand-alone exercise or skill set. The authors suggest *students* also benefit from understanding how knowledge and processes are structured. Specific strategies are offered that honor students' personal intellect and help them consciously apply knowledge and skills to construct their own conceptual schemas.

Since textbooks and purchased instructional units are generally not Concept Based, it is critical that teachers use the principles outlined in this and other books on Concept-Based Curriculum to design instructional units and lessons. Stern, Ferraro, and Mohnkern provide clear models, frameworks, and examples for designing Concept-Based lessons. Their four lesson frameworks bring together, through examples, the essential tenets of student-centered, intellectually engaging, Concept-Based pedagogy.

The authors address assessment for conceptual understanding—an area that has been slow to evolve. It is easy to assess content and lower level skills, but assessing for transferable, conceptual understanding often feels nebulous—hard to nail down. Thankfully, assessment is changing. This book provides teachers with the rationale and specific methods for assessing beyond the facts and lower level skills. The chapter on assessment is both enlightening and timely in today's test-driven environment.

Ensuring equity in learning is a fundamental right of every student. This book helps teachers evaluate their instruction for equitable learning opportunities in four critical areas:

- Teacher expectations and relationships with students
- Purposeful and clear goals, activities, instructions and assessments
- Constant collection of evidence, effective feedback, and thoughtful goal setting by teacher and students, and
- Flexible grouping based on what students need at that moment to reach the goal.

These areas have always been a focus for educators, but they require laser-like, minds-on work when considered in Concept-Based classrooms. Each of these areas needs to reflect the practices of *Concept-Based* teaching and learning with equitable opportunities and outcomes in mind.

Finally, the authors of this book help teachers understand the relationship between popular educational initiatives and various academic standards relative to

Concept-Based Curriculum and Instruction. Stern, Ferraro, and Mohnkern have written a coherent and cohesive book to support teachers as they shift from a traditional model to the cutting-edge Concept-Based model, which raises the bar for both instructional pedagogy and student performance. You will enjoy the Concept-Based learning journey with the support of this book. It may take effort, but the rewards will be plentiful—especially as you begin to see attributes of intellectual development blossom in your students, attributes like those of the tenacious and inquiring Maisie Dobbs, who would never accept quick, easy answers and who values reflection, emotions, and deep grappling as essentials of learning and to unraveling life's mysteries!

—*H. Lynn Erickson and Lois A. Lanning*

Acknowledgments

The authors would like to thank Dr. H. Lynn Erickson and Dr. Lois A. Lanning for their vision and dedication to creating both theoretical explanations and concrete tools for designing curriculum and instruction for deep understanding. Their mentorship over the past several years has been an incredible gift. We admire you and we thank you.

To Ariel Bartlett, for your enthusiasm and sage advice. We are extremely grateful. And to the design team at Corwin, thank you for making this book look beautiful.

To the teachers and students at Cesar Chavez Public Charter Schools for Public Policy in Washington, D.C. (from 2007 to 2015), you taught us more about teaching, curriculum design, and leadership than you will know.

To Mrs. Irasema Salcido, for your vision and for your continued support.

To Dr. Sheron Brown, for introducing us to the work of Dr. Erickson, the Foundation for Critical Thinking, and lots of other great work on deep learning.

To the teachers, leaders, and students at Colegio Anglo Colombiano in Bogotá, Colombia, for your openness to experimentation with these ideas and for your belief in possibility.

To our husbands, Josh, Craig, and Brett, for your love, support, artwork, and edits.

To our families, especially Gordon and Justine Harris, Michael and Karen Stern, Alex Tolor, Hannah Robinson, and Lois Schwartz, for your support, encouragement, babysitting, proofreading, and edits.

And to Julie's two boys, Alex and Andrew, for your patience as mommy got this done. Hopefully your schools will have deep, conceptual learning at the heart of the curriculum.

Publisher's Acknowledgments

Corwin gratefully acknowledges the following reviewers for their editorial insight and guidance:

Brenda Booth, Instructional Coach
Burlington-Edison School District
Burlington, WA

Julia Briggs, Science Teacher
Colegio Anglo Colombiano
Bogotá Distrito Capital, Colombia

Georgina Alice Carey, Chemistry Teacher
(Grades 6–9)
Colegio Anglo Colombiano
Bogotá Distrito Capital, Colombia

Elita Driskill, Educational Consultant/
Coach
Education Service Center, Region 11
White Settlement, TX

Fraser Halliwell, Director of Secondary
School
Colegio Anglo Colombiano
Bogotá Distrito Capital, Colombia

Richard Healy, Deputy Director of
Secondary School, English Language
and Literature Teacher, Theory of
Knowledge Teacher
Colegio Anglo Colombiano
Bogotá Distrito Capital, Colombia

Jane Hunn, General Science Teacher
(Grade 6)
Tippecanoe Valley Middle School
Akron, IN

Neville Kirton, Director of the
Humanities Department
Colegio Anglo Colombiano
Bogotá Distrito Capital, Colombia

Susanne Long, Director of Curriculum,
Research, and Development Services
Onslow County Schools
Jacksonville, NC

Ayo Magwood, Social Studies
Teacher
Maret School
Washington, DC

Amanda McKee, Secondary Mathematics
Teacher
Johnsonville High School
Johnsonville, SC

Lyneille Meza, Director of Data and
Assessment
Denton Independent School District
Denton, TX

Amy Reisner, Assistant Principal (K-8),
District Concept-Based Trainer
Bay View Elementary
Burlington, WA

Ms. Mona Seervai, Principal
Bombay International School
Mumbai, India

About the Authors

Julie Stern is a teacher trainer and instructional coach, supporting schools in transforming teaching and learning on four continents. She is passionate about helping educators to maximize human potential and break free of the long-standing industrial model of schooling. Julie is a certified trainer in Concept-Based Curriculum and Instruction and served as a specialist for Dr. H. Lynn Erickson's Concept-Based Curriculum and Instruction Certification Institutes. She is a James Madison Constitutional Scholar and taught social studies for many years at schools in the Northeast and her native Louisiana. She is a Verified Master Trainer and has Coaching and Change Management Certificates from the Association for Talent Development (ATD). Julie previously served as the director of Public Policy and Curriculum Innovation at the Cesar Chavez Public Charter Schools in Washington, DC, where she led the revision of curriculum in all subject areas for Grades 6 through 12. She has a master's degree in international education from The George Washington University and a bachelor's degree in sociology and psychology from Loyola University New Orleans. She currently resides in Bogotá, Colombia, with her husband, a U.S. diplomat, and two young sons.

Krista Ferraro is the History Department head at Thayer Academy in Braintree, Massachusetts. She is passionate about social justice and civic education. Previously, she served as the deputy director of Public Policy and Curriculum Innovation as well as a history teacher at Cesar Chavez Public Charter Schools in Washington, DC, where she repeatedly led her students to winning the DC We the People Constitution competition. Krista began her career in education as a 2006 Teach for America corps member. She holds a master's degree in teaching from American University and a bachelor's degree in American studies and Spanish from Cornell University.

 **Juliet Mohnkern** is the director of High Tech Middle North County in San Diego, California. In 2015, she completed an MEd in Educational Leadership at the High Tech High Graduate School of Education. She is passionate about providing all students with equitable access to learning that is academically rigorous, meaningful to students, and impactful in the real world. Previously, she was the director of Public Policy and Curriculum Innovation at Cesar Chavez Public Charter Schools in Washington, DC. She also worked at Match Charter Public School in Boston, Massachusetts. She has a master's degree in ethics, peace, and global affairs from American University and a bachelor's degree in classics from Boston College.

In 2013, Julie, Krista, and Juliet cofounded Education to Save the World (www.edtosavetheworld.com), pushing for a vision of schooling where learning is organized around real-world problems that require the flexible application of each subjects' concepts and skills to create a more sustainable, just, and healthy planet. Their summer workshops draw teachers and leaders from around the world to collaborate on ways to transform teaching and learning to meet the demands of the 21st century.

Introduction

*Why Is Concept-Based Curriculum
Critical for the 21st Century?*

Educators today seem to be faced with a choice: Continue teaching centuries-old ways of organizing the world through traditional disciplines such as mathematics and music or throw them out in favor of innovation and creativity in order to move into a 21st-century paradigm for teaching and learning.

This is a false choice. Here's the important truth: Innovation requires the creative transfer of the fundamental and powerful concepts of the traditional disciplines. We should put real-world challenges in front of students that require them to improvise based on what humanity has already discovered. Innovators stand on the shoulders of past scientists and mathematicians in order to innovate. They don't invent without a deep understanding of how the world works.

Innovation occurs when people creatively *transfer* what they learn to complex situations. It relies on abstracting to a conceptual level in order to do it. Although innovation is a current buzz word, the imperative to design education in this way stands on a long history of research.

> Innovation requires the creative transfer of the fundamental and powerful concepts of the traditional disciplines.

Decades ago, cognitive psychologist Jerome Bruner (1977) wrote, "Grasping the structure of a subject is understanding it in a way that permits many other things to be related to it meaningfully" (p. 7). He wrote this at a gathering of leading scientists who were tasked with figuring out how to improve schooling in the United States after the Soviets launched Sputnik. These experts wanted schools to produce innovators and concluded that conceptual understanding was the way to achieve that goal.

Nearly 20 years ago, corporate analyst Teresa Amabile (1998) explained in *Harvard Business Review,* "Within every individual, creativity is a function of three components: expertise, creative-thinking skills, and motivation" (p. 81). Students still need a depth of knowledge and understanding in order to innovate. Amabile's research echoes what Bruner posited decades earlier: It would be unwise to throw out the academic disciplines and replace them with the goal of innovation without the support of a deep knowledge base.

We need knowledge in order to innovate—but facts alone are not sufficient. Academic standards attempt to articulate the knowledge and skills our students need as a foundation for an educated populace. This approach, however, typically lacks a focus on the organizing framework of that knowledge. It needs a conceptual skeleton to give it shape. Disconnected pieces of knowledge are not particularly useful in the era of innovation. Expertise requires that knowledge be organized in the brain in order to be employed to create something new.

> Disconnected pieces of knowledge are not particularly useful in the era of innovation.

In its landmark publication on learning, the National Research Council (Bransford, 2000) explained, "To develop competence in an area of inquiry, students must understand facts and ideas in the context of a conceptual framework" (p. 12). This is what separates experts from novices. A beginner in any field has to work hard to memorize what seem like disparate pieces of information while an advanced practitioner stores knowledge in associated categories, something like a giant filing cabinet in the brain. Yet today's standards and curricula are not typically organized in the context of a conceptual framework. And educators rarely make this organization explicit to students.

The revised Bloom's taxonomy—a taxonomy for learning, teaching, and assessing (Anderson & Krathwohl, 2001)—asks, "Is mathematics, for example, a discrete body of knowledge to be memorized or an organized, coherent, conceptual system to be understood?" (p. 6). The answer is clearly the latter, but too often we teach mathematics as if it's a list of unrelated operations, a series of steps to be learned and applied with limited understanding.

Nearly 30 years ago, Perkins and Salomon (1988) reported, "[T]ransfer always involves reflective thought in abstracting from one context and seeking connections with others" (p. 26). They pointed to the problem of overly contextualized or "local" knowledge that does not ask students to abstract to broader ideas. "The most artful instructional design will not provoke transfer if the knowledge and skills in question are fundamentally local in character, not really transferable to other contexts in the first place" (Perkins & Salomon, 1988, p. 28). In other words, we must organize our curriculum around abstract concepts to promote transfer to unfamiliar contexts.

Most recently, the work of education researchers Fisher, Frey, and Hattie (2016) recognized the importance of conceptual thinking to transfer learning to complex situations. "As students deepen their learning, we look for them to think in increasingly conceptual ways" (p. 112). Hattie's thorough meta-analysis demonstrates that organizing conceptual knowledge is a particularly powerful strategy with an enormous impact on student learning (Hattie, 2012).

Consider this sample assessment from a sixth-grade social studies class. Students encountered this situation for the first time on their final exam. The following image demonstrates the shrinking of the Aral Sea in Central Asia between 1989 and 2014.

It was once the fourth largest lake on Earth and was essential for the livelihood of thousands of people. Soviet irrigation projects devastated the lake, inciting a migrant crisis as residents fled Uzbekistan in the hope of employment in Kazakhstan (see Figure 0.1).

FIGURE 0.1   THE DISAPPEARANCE OF THE ARAL SEA

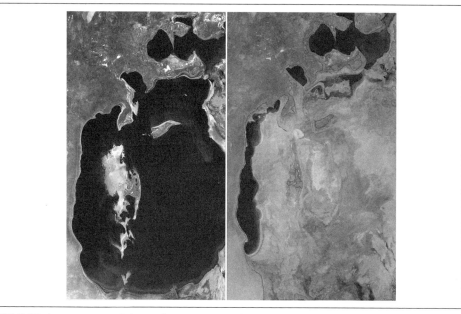

SOURCE: A comparison of the Aral Sea in 1989 (left) and 2014 (right). Image by NASA, collage by Producercunningham (2014), Public Domain. https://en.wikipedia.org/wiki/Aral_Sea#/media/File:Aral Sea1989_2014.jpg.

Students were required to use their understanding of transferable concepts such as migration, hardship, resources, and opportunity to unlock this new, complex situation. The topic of the unit was U.S. westward migration, but instead of remaining at the factual and topical level, the students used the facts of the unit to answer transferable, conceptual questions such as, "What is the relationship between migration, resources, and opportunity?" and "Does migration ever come with hardship?" By answering these conceptual questions as they studied U.S. westward migration, students were better prepared to unlock other situations involving migration such as the Aral Sea crisis.

The work cited earlier only scratches the surface of the research that highlights the importance of developing students' conceptual frameworks. It also only begins to tell the story of how our current approach to teaching and learning largely ignores this critical element. While there are a number of good tools to guide curriculum writing in the name of deep understanding, the work of H. Lynn Erickson and Lois A. Lanning provides the most detailed explanations, definitions, and tools to guide us toward learning that builds an organizational understanding of the disciplines and allows students to unlock the myriad new situations they will encounter.

This book builds on the foundation provided by Erickson and Lanning and is intended to provide secondary teachers with more detailed tools and resources for the daily activities of the classroom. Readers will find more value in this book if they have already read one of Erickson and Lanning's works and have drafted unit plans using their principles and tools.

Concept-Based series books:

- *Concept-Based Curriculum and Instruction for the Thinking Classroom* (Erickson, Lanning, & French, 2017, 2nd ed.)
- *Concept-Based Mathematics: Teaching for Deep Understanding in Secondary Classrooms* (Wathall, 2016)
- *Transitioning to Concept-Based Curriculum and Instruction* (Erickson & Lanning, 2014)
- *Designing a Concept-Based Curriculum for English Language Arts* (Lanning, 2013)
- *Stirring the Head, Heart, and Soul* (Erickson, 2008, 3rd ed.)

There is a second false dichotomy floating around education circles these days. It is very trendy to emphasize the importance of certain disciplines such as STEM (science, technology, engineering, and mathematics) over the liberal arts. This is an unnecessary choice. The world is interdisciplinary. How can we expect students to solve multifaceted problems like international conflict over scarce resources and a global rise in terrorism without a deep understanding of concepts such as power, scarcity, and conflict, as well as essential competencies such as media literacy and analysis of multiple perspectives gained from a liberal arts education? Abstracting to the conceptual level is key for understanding problems and creating solutions that draw on multiple disciplines. And this type of learning is essential for the issues facing this generation of students.

Motivation is another key component for teaching and learning in the era of innovation. Students need to persevere in the face of obstacles and commit to a life of learning. Again, abstracting to the conceptual level of thought helps us achieve this goal. Erickson (2008) noticed a pattern from early childhood education through secondary school: As conceptual understanding decreases and the amount of factual recall increases, student motivation for learning plummets. She explained that when we engage students on a conceptual level, motivation soars because the brain naturally seeks to make connections and discover patterns.

For example, the study of history becomes much more interesting if students try to recognize patterns about freedom, leadership, and conflict. Learning science is more intriguing when looking to figure out how changing one part of a system impacts the other parts. And reading literature takes on new meaning when discovering why authors choose certain literary devices and analyzing their effects on readers.

Erickson and Lanning (2014) explained:

> Synergistic thinking requires the interaction of factual knowledge and concepts. Synergistic thinking requires a deeper level of mental processing and leads to increased understanding of facts related to concepts, supports personal meaning-making, and increases motivation for learning. It is motivating to use our minds well! (p. 36)

Here are some quotes from students:

> "It's been challenging, but we learn more. Last year we did lots of things but this year we do more concept work. They allow us to reach a deeper understanding of what we're learning. They let us transfer our understanding to other situations."
>
> —Grade 8 student

> "I love it! At first I felt worried because I didn't write down a lot of notes in class. But as I left the classroom I thought, 'I really understand and can remember the meaning of "absorption" and "assimilation" without having to go back and study my notes.'"
>
> —Grade 11 student

The trouble is, the longer students are in school with a traditional, fact-centered curriculum, the more effort we have to make to change their mindsets about what learning is and should be. That is why this book is focused on secondary students—the older they are, the more work we have to do! Resist the temptation of skipping over the strategies found in Chapter 2, which lays the foundation for a thinking classroom. It is an investment that will pay off handsomely.

Trust us—we learned the hard way. We attempted to introduce a Concept-Based Curriculum in a set of schools that, for the most part, were really stuck at the surface level of learning; fact and skill drills were the order of the day. When we tried to jump over setting the foundation for intellectual work, the students rejected the notion of deeper levels of thinking, saying it was too difficult and that we were not actually teaching them—because we were not spoon-feeding the information to them. When we told them the goal was intellectual growth, using the strategies found here, everything changed. They put more effort into their learning and their sense of pride in themselves as intellectual beings skyrocketed.

Finally, we must note that too often, rather than truly transforming education, schools make small changes that wrap up old goals in new practices. For example, a lot of "innovative" schooling practices emphasize a personalized approach to learning where students move at their own pace, slowing down when they need more help or practice and speeding up when they are ready to move on, even if their peers are not. This is great practice. But we wonder: What good is personalized learning if the goals of the learning remain stuck in covering facts and skills without depth of understanding?

> Too often, rather than truly transforming education, schools make small changes that wrap up old goals in new practices.

Building a Concept-Based Curriculum is a major and likely the best first step toward transforming school for the 21st century. Education fads come and go. Most arise from good intentions and many have positive attributes. We are advocates of and trainers for several educational initiatives. We think each has merit and that a great school hits them all, even if it's very difficult to pull off.

But no other single initiative does more to raise both intellectual rigor and student motivation while also honoring the traditional disciplines *and* preparing students to tackle problems they've never seen before. That's the power of Concept-Based Curriculum and Instruction. We need to transform the goals of teaching and learning (curriculum) and not simply change the delivery method (instruction). When we organize our curriculum through fundamental and powerful concepts, our students are able to transfer their understanding to new situations and apply it in unique ways. In this way they create something innovative and world-changing, becoming the next great innovators.

Chapter Overview

Chapter 1 of this book provides a review of Erickson and Lanning's work to refresh readers' memories and emphasize key points. Specific unit planning steps can be found in this chapter.

Chapter 2 sets the stage for deeper learning and presents concrete strategies to reorient secondary students—who often need quite a bit of coaching—on how to monitor and improve their own thinking. We have found it to be a worthy investment of time to teach students the value of this type of learning because it is often very different from what they have experienced. When teachers skip this step, they and their students can easily become frustrated.

Chapters 3 and 4 are the heart of the book, providing several concrete strategies for introducing concepts in the disciplines and guiding students toward their own formulation of conceptual relationships. Chapter 3 contains important explanations and strategies for helping students uncover conceptual relationships. Chapter 4 provides four distinct lesson frameworks to guide lesson design. We have provided guiding questions and sample activities but we hope teachers will use their creativity and experience to bring these lesson frameworks to life.

Chapter 5 illustrates important principles and related strategies for designing ongoing, formative assessments for conceptual understanding. These assessments, paired with positive feedback, are essential in providing information to both teacher and student about progress and insight into what to do next.

Chapter 6 promotes principles and strategies toward creating an equitable classroom through differentiation, challenging low expectations and other methods. Concept-Based Curriculum naturally lends itself to more equity for students. We want to take this a step further by offering additional strategies. We feel passionately about the need to consciously and deliberately work on unraveling the long tradition of inequality of schools. This chapter only scratches the surface, but we hope it will spur reflection and provide tools to aid teachers in this important pursuit.

Chapter 7 is designed to help teachers digest the relationship between Concept-Based Curriculum and several other initiatives and priorities. If your school is like all those we've worked with, you likely have multiple goals or initiatives you or your administrators are trying to integrate to provide what's best for students. We feel that those of us who have time to read and reflect need to help busy teachers digest, correlate, and implement what often feels like an overwhelming amount of new ideas or changes.

The conclusion to our book lays out a concrete picture of what school could look like if conceptual understanding was at the center of lesson planning and students used their learning to solve real-world problems. This book provides tools, ideas, and strategies to guide teachers in creating classrooms that foster deep, conceptual, transferable learning. We sincerely hope you find it useful.

....

CHAPTER 1

What Are the Essential Elements of Concept-Based Curriculum Design?

Deep learning, big ideas, "Aha!" moments—most educators aim for a level of comprehension that moves beyond simple memorization. We want our students to not only retain what we've taught them but relate it to other things they encounter, using each new situation to add nuance and sophistication to their thinking. We want to empower them and foster a love of learning. Along with dozens of teachers we know, we have spent countless hours trying to find strategies that build a depth of understanding. But we also know from a mountain of research that the average classroom has remained remarkably unchanged over the past 100 years. The content addressed and level of thinking required continue to largely remain at the surface level (Hattie, 2012; Mehta & Fine, 2015).

Why is there such a considerable gap between aspirations for deep learning and classroom reality? This is the million-dollar question—and we don't want to oversimplify the answer. But we believe that a big factor is a lack of practical, concrete tools for teachers. The methods created by H. Lynn Erickson and Lois A. Lanning are the most powerful and clear ways to design curriculum to allow students to transfer their learning to new contexts. This chapter provides a review of their work and is intended to emphasize key points about unit planning before we move into lesson planning and formative assessments. For more in-depth coverage of these topics, we recommend that educators reference the latest book coauthored by Erickson, Lanning, and French: *Concept-Based Curriculum and Instruction for the Thinking Classroom* (2017).

This chapter reinforces the following principles of Concept-Based Curriculum design:

- The traditional coverage-based curriculum model, which relies on students "doing" verbs with content, rarely produces deep or transferable learning.

- Concept-Based units focus on using content—topics, facts, and skills—to investigate the relationship among concepts.

- Uncovering the relationship among concepts produces learning that can transfer to new situations and helps students unlock novel problems.

- Planning a Concept-Based unit requires teachers to engage in synergistic thinking—the cognitive interplay between the lower and conceptual levels of thinking—to discern the concepts and conceptual relationships at the heart of the unit; there are no shortcuts.

- Concept-Based planning requires that time and effort be devoted to crafting, revising, and polishing factual, conceptual, and debatable questions.

Knowledge and Understanding

The first important distinction is the one Erickson and Lanning make between traditional, coverage-centered curriculum and one that fosters deeper levels of understanding. What does that mean, exactly, to go beyond surface levels of knowing?

One of the most powerful pieces of research in education is Anderson and Krathwohl's *A Taxonomy for Learning, Teaching, and Assessing* (2001). Nearly every trained educator has some knowledge of Bloom's taxonomy and the hierarchy of different types of thinking—from recall to analysis or synthesis. The first taxonomy was published in the 1950s. Many educators also know that there is a revised Bloom's taxonomy, created by a team led by Lorin Anderson, who worked closely with Bloom on the original version. Figure 1.1 demonstrates how the revised version made minor changes to the *thinking hierarchy,* such as replacing "knowledge" with "remembering" and replacing "synthesis" with "creating," which it now places at the highest point.

FIGURE 1.1   BLOOM'S TAXONOMY REVISION

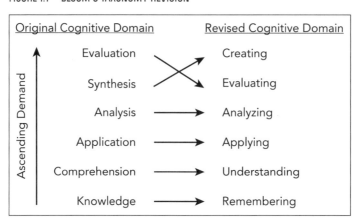

Adapted from Anderson & Krathwohl (2001).

Most educators are familiar with this shift, which reminds teachers that creating new knowledge is the most demanding cognitive process, while simple recall is the least demanding. Fewer educators, though, have considered the other major change to Bloom's taxonomy: the *knowledge dimension*. Anderson and Krathwohl (2001) took "knowledge" out of the cognitive domain and added it as a separate dimension, recognizing four distinct types: factual, conceptual, procedural, and metacognitive.

See the full taxonomy revision in Figure 1.2. Notice that instead of six ways to think about one type of knowledge, there are six ways to think about four distinct types of knowledge. This is key!

FIGURE 1.2 ANDERSON AND KRATHWOHL'S (2001) COGNITIVE AND KNOWLEDGE DIMENSIONS

Knowledge Dimension	Cognitive Process Dimension					
	Remember	Understand	Apply	Analyze	Evaluate	Create
Factual Knowledge						
Conceptual Knowledge						
Procedural Knowledge						
Metacognitive Knowledge						

SOURCE: Anderson, L. W., & Krathwohl, D. R. (2001). *A taxonomy for learning, teaching, and assessing: A revision of Bloom's taxonomy of educational objectives.* New York: Longman.

What is most important for Concept-Based teachers to take away from this revised taxonomy?

- This is further, rigorous research that supports the importance of helping students organize information and make connections between abstract concepts to gain more insight into the disciplines. Simply trying to match higher ordered thinking skills with facts is not going to produce deep learning that transfers.

- Erickson uses slightly different terminology: Facts correspond to knowledge and concepts correspond to *understanding*. Factual knowledge doesn't transfer but conceptual understanding does.

- Instructional strategies should match the knowledge type and cognitive process of the learning goal. For instance, if the goal is for students to remember facts, teachers may ask students to use a mnemonic device. But if the goal is to apply concepts, this strategy won't work.

- Assessments should align to the knowledge types and cognitive processes taught. Teachers are bound to get poor results when their instruction is mainly at the remembering, factual level, but their assessments demand that students evaluate conceptual ideas.

The new taxonomy is useful in many ways. We love how it reminds teachers to be strategic about both *how* they want students to think (the cognitive dimension) and *what* they want students to think about (the knowledge dimension).

The taxonomy also has its limitations. For instance, it does very little to illuminate the *relationship* among facts, concepts, procedures, and metacognitive awareness. While a hierarchical relationship among cognitive processes is implied, the knowledge dimension does not provide much insight into the nature of each type of knowledge and even gives the false sense that facts, concepts, procedures, and metacognition are completely separate entities. Let's take a look at Erickson's depiction of the Structure of Knowledge, which predates the revised taxonomy. It is simpler than the revised taxonomy and offers greater insight into the *relationship* between factual knowledge and conceptual understanding.

The Structure of Knowledge

Using a very straightforward and powerful graphic, Erickson shows us how knowledge is structured and provides a visual that helps us to see the *interplay* between factual knowledge and conceptual understanding. Review Figure 1.3 and notice the choice of language here. While Anderson and Krathwohl use the term "knowledge" to describe both facts and concepts, Erickson reminds us of the need to distinguish between factual *knowledge* and conceptual *understanding*. The Structure of Knowledge visual also reminds us that conceptual understanding is built by abstracting "up" from factual knowledge or examples to understand the relationship among concepts.

FIGURE 1.3   ERICKSON'S STRUCTURE OF KNOWLEDGE

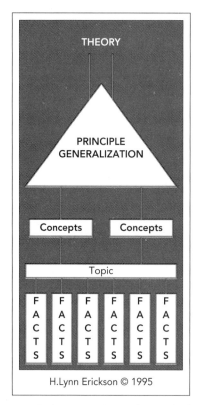

H. Lynn Erickson © 1995

SOURCE: Erickson, H. L. (2008). *Stirring the head, heart, and soul: Redefining curriculum, instruction, and concept-based learning* (3rd ed.). Thousand Oaks, CA: Corwin.

Upon reflection, we can easily see how most curriculum design models stop at the topical level. For instance, many curriculum documents list learning goals and activities related to the Enlightenment in social studies, the digestive system in science, or three-dimensional shapes in geometry. Typically, these topics frame a set of facts. Both the topics and facts are locked in time, place, and/or situation. And although they are often paired with a thinking skill—*identify, analyze, evaluate, solve*—they are too specific to allow students to transfer their learning to new situations. When exposed to this type of curriculum, some students are able to abstract to the conceptual level on their own, generalizing about how *intellectual movements* work in social studies after studying the Enlightenment, how *systems* work in science after studying the digestive system, or how *volume* works in mathematics after learning the equation $V = \frac{4}{3}\pi r^3$, but we should not and cannot leave this to chance.

Some curriculum documents go further up the Structure of Knowledge to the level of concepts: change, pattern, systems. Concepts are mental constructs that are abstract, timeless, and universal (Erickson & Lanning, 2014, p. 33). They transfer to multiple situations. But what allows students to transfer their understanding to new situations is the *relationship* between two or more concepts, known in Erickson's work as generalizations or principles. To emphasize the importance of this point, we will refer to these as statements of conceptual relationship or, simply, conceptual relationships.

> **What allows students to transfer their understanding to new situations is the *relationship* between two or more concepts.**

The importance of the conceptual relationship level (principles and generalizations) on the Structure of Knowledge cannot be overemphasized. Students must understand two or more concepts and state them *in relation* to one another. If students can define and identify change or patterns but not understand them in relation to other universal or disciplinary concepts, they will still struggle to solve a complex problem involving change or patterns in the future.

Erickson and Lanning (2014) made another important distinction about different types of concepts. Concepts such as change, pattern, and system are extremely broad and can be applied across disciplines—for this reason they are called macroconcepts. Many educators hope students will make connections across disciplines, and this is certainly a very worthy goal. At the same time, we want to note that the beauty of Concept-Based Curriculum is that it includes the ability to transfer ideas *within* the disciplines. More disciplinary-specific ideas are called microconcepts. We need microconcepts to achieve disciplinary depth (pp. 40–41).

Consider the example of a common beginning algebra unit, Straight-Line Graphs, in Figure 1.4. Think about how the *statements of conceptual relationship* allow students to transfer understanding of straight-line graphs to new situations within the discipline of mathematics. Knowing the definitions of the concepts on their own is not enough.

And consider the example in Figure 1.5 from a typical social studies curriculum. Most curriculum documents will outline the key examples (facts) and topics to be studied, and it may be obvious to students that the concepts of freedom and conflict lie at the heart of the situation. But think about the difference between asking questions about concepts (*How does the story of "Bleeding Kansas" relate to conflict?*) and asking questions about the *relationship* between concepts (*How does "Bleeding Kansas"*

FIGURE 1.4 CONCEPTUAL RELATIONSHIPS IN ALGEBRA

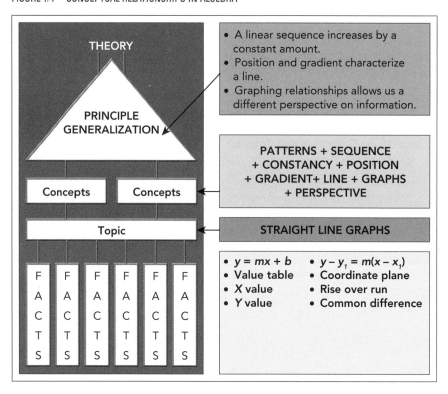

FIGURE 1.5 CONCEPTUAL RELATIONSHIPS IN SOCIAL STUDIES

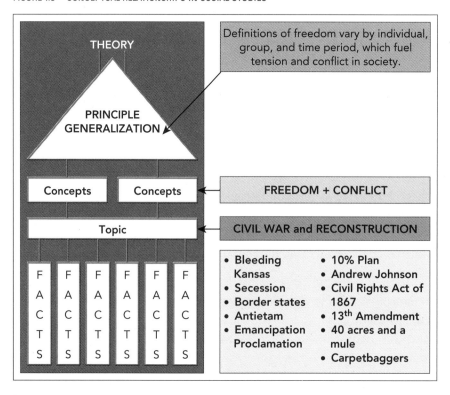

*help us understand the larger relationship between **freedom** and **conflict?**)*. The latter is a much more powerful tool for illuminating meaning that applies across time, place, and situation. Understanding that different views of freedom fuel conflict can help students better understand everything from the spread of ISIS in the Middle East to their own battles over curfew times.

Erickson's Structure of Knowledge and corresponding definitions show us how facts, which are concrete and specific, relate to other key components of a good curriculum: topics, concepts and conceptual relationships.

Clarifying Transfer: The Ultimate Goal of Concept-Based Curriculum and Instruction

Whenever we ask teachers *why* students need to know what they're teaching, we get a variety of answers. For some, the topics or facts seem important in and of themselves. "Kids *must* read and learn *Hamlet* because it's one of the most significant and well-known literary works in existence," an English teacher may say. But, most often, we hear teachers say that the content they teach should help students lead productive lives in the future. They want students to be strong thinkers, problem solvers, readers, writers, and speakers. They want kids to see the world differently, and to be empowered to act differently, because of what they have learned. It seems that the goal of all learning—not just Concept-Based learning—is transfer.

The key to understanding transfer is this: Facts and topics do not transfer. By this we mean that facts and topics cannot be applied directly to a new situation. Whenever we try to apply our insights from one situation to another we are *always* abstracting to the conceptual level, generalizing from a specific instance to a broader rule, before our knowledge helps us unlock the new situation.

> The key to understanding transfer is this: Facts and topics do not transfer.

Our brains are wired for this process. A toddler, after tasting peas and broccoli, is hesitant to try spinach; he has created a generalization that relates taste and color to help guide his decisions when faced with a new vegetable. Another child predicts that the princess will be rescued from the clutches of the evil queen after watching several Disney movies where "good triumphs over evil." We move naturally between factual instances and the conceptual rules or patterns that make up the logic of our world.

The problem is, if we remain at the topic and factual level, students stop trying to derive larger principles about what they're learning. By the time they reach middle school, they have been conditioned to retrieve knowledge on cue without deep understanding. But we continue to expect transfer. Knowing that students read *Hamlet* last year, we assume they will have more insight into *Romeo and Juliet*. Once they've learned to perform calculations involving fractions, we expect them to solve a word problem that asks them to cut a recipe in half or to double it. We're surprised when learning doesn't transfer in these ways. Too often, we assign students a poor grade and move on.

The great thing about conceptual learning is that it makes visible and concrete the process by which we turn our knowledge of facts into transferable, conceptual understandings. If students use their reading of *Hamlet* to investigate the relationship between the concepts of free will and fate, spending considerable time refining their generalizations about these concepts, they will more readily recognize their generalizations at work when they read *Romeo and Juliet*. And when young math students use their study of fractions to investigate the relationship between multiplication and division, rather than just memorizing the algorithms, they are more capable of attacking a tough word problem where the appropriate algorithm is not obvious.

These are examples of *academic transfer,* meaning the transfer of understanding from one school assignment to the next. When we talk about transfer of learning in this book, we are also talking about *transfer to real-world situations or problems.* This means that students' understanding of conceptual relationships should alter how they see the world *beyond* the walls of the classroom and how they solve problems that occur outside the neat, teacher-constructed parameters of an academic exercise. For us, the ultimate goal is not just to transfer understanding from the study of *Hamlet* to the study of *Othello.* It's great for students to understand how views of free will and fate impact the characters of these plays, but it's even better when they can apply these insights to solving, say, the high school dropout crisis by recognizing that students' decisions to drop out are related to the degree to which they see themselves as fated to fail.

Notice that *conceptual transfer* is different from *making connections.* Teachers often ask students to make topical or factual connections to extend learning and make it meaningful. For instance, when her class is studying the impact of drugs on the body, a health teacher may ask students to read articles about the problem of opioid addiction and decide whether they would support a law that prohibited doctors from prescribing opioid medicines for periods longer than five days. Clearly, students must draw on what they know to respond to this assignment. But they are not asked to draw on *concepts;* rather, they are asked to rely on facts about the topic of drug addiction. Conceptual transfer only occurs when students apply insights about the relationship among concepts to a new scenario.

> Conceptual transfer only occurs when students apply insights about the relationship among concepts to a new scenario.

Educational researcher John Hattie's (2012) work supports the claim that conceptual understanding is key to transferring learning to new situations:

> We come to know ideas, and then we can be asked to relate and extend them. This leads to conceptual understanding, which can in turn become a new idea—and so the cycle continues. These conceptual

understandings form the "coat hangers" on which we interpret and assimilate new ideas, and relate and extend them. (p. 115)

Hattie (2012) said there are three distinct levels of learning: surface, deep, and transfer, as shown in Figure 1.6. All three levels are essential, and we reiterate that point later in the section titled "Synergistic Thinking." Hattie and his coauthors stated, "Together, surface and deep understanding lead to the student developing conceptual understanding" (Fisher et al., 2016, p. 61). They agreed that "the ultimate goal, and one that is hard to realize, is transfer. When students reach this level, learning has been accomplished" (Fisher et al., 2016, p. 19).

FIGURE 1.6   SURFACE, DEEP, AND TRANSFER LEARNING

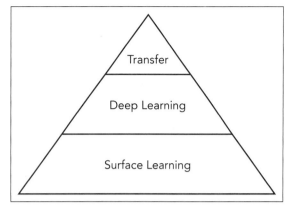

SOURCE: Fisher, D., Frey, N., & Hattie, J. (2016).

In the 1980s, researchers Perkins and Salomon (1988) coined a distinction between what they call low-road transfer and high-road transfer. Essentially, when tasks remain similar to one another, this is known as low-road transfer. When students are asked to transfer knowledge to dissimilar tasks, which requires them to increasingly generalize concepts, they are performing high-road transfer. For those who agree that the 21st century demands innovation, this thinking by the titans in educational

FIGURE 1.7   REAL-WORLD HIGH-ROAD TRANSFER

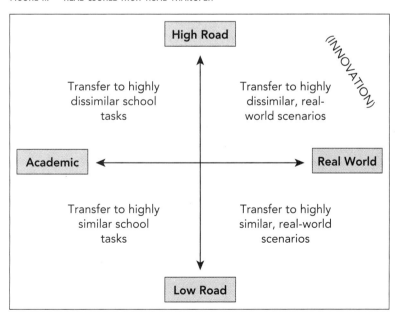

SOURCE: © Stern, Ferraro, and Mohnkern, (2016).

> Innovation is high-road, real-world transfer of learning. And it is done at the conceptual level.

research cannot be ignored. Innovation is high-road, real-world transfer of learning. And it is done at the conceptual level.

We've combined Perkins and Salomon's high-road and low-road transfer with our academic and real-world transfer to illustrate the key to fostering innovation. Formal schooling needs to live in all four quadrants because a deep foundation of facts or surface-level learning is key for deep learning, transfer, and innovation. But the point is that the upper right quadrant is where innovation happens, as shown on the previous page in Figure 1.7. And we will show you how to reach it!

The Structure of Process

Lois A. Lanning is an expert in the field of literacy. She points out that there is a difference among the traditional subjects or disciplines taught in schools. Some are more knowledge based, such as mathematics, science, and social studies, each with their own set of facts that were discovered by experts in the field. Other disciplines are more process based, focused on processes, strategies, and skills rather than concrete knowledge. In these disciplines, the experts apply a complex process to *produce* an end result. These are language, music, theater, dance, and visual arts.

Teachers of these subjects sometimes try to shoehorn their content into the knowledge-based model, leading them to focus their instruction on the characters and plots of Shakespeare, the colors and shapes of Picasso's Blue Period, or in-depth analysis of Mozart's symphonies. These are important elements to any arts curriculum. But the heart of the curriculum is the complex process that the experts in the fields *do:* the writing process, the artistic process.

This relates directly back to the revised Bloom's taxonomy, which separates procedural knowledge from the three other types of knowledge. Anderson and Krathwohl (2001) described procedural knowledge as "the knowledge of skills, algorithms, techniques, and methods," as well as "knowledge of the criteria used to determine when to use various procedures" (p. 52). This would include the research process in social studies, the scientific method in science, various methods of literary criticism in English language arts, and the steps involved in asserting a geometric proof in mathematics. However, Anderson and Krathwohl do not fully explain what it takes for students to transfer their knowledge of procedures to new situations.

Lanning offers a visual that shows how skills and strategies make up more complex processes, which can be abstracted to statements of conceptual relationship. She explains that understanding conceptual relationships helps students "move from 'doing' to 'understanding' *why* we do what we do" (Erickson & Lanning, 2014, p. 44).

For instance, students who understand that *writers introduce and respond to counterarguments in order to make their own claims more convincing* are more likely to transfer the strategies and skills associated with making counterarguments to new situations because they understand *why* this is important and how strong counterarguments are constructed.

In the same way that Erickson's Structure of Knowledge makes clear the relationship between factual knowledge and conceptual understanding, Lanning's Structure of Process, shown in Figure 1.8, makes clear the relationship between processes and conceptual understanding.

Erickson and Lanning (2014) noted that, although some disciplines are more process oriented than others, "we should consider both knowledge and processes when designing concept-based curricula" no matter the discipline (p. 49). Obviously, the balance between knowledge and processes will depend on the nature of the discipline itself. This is why Lanning's work on the Structure of Process is so important. Process is, to varying degrees, an essential component of every discipline.

FIGURE 1.8 LANNING'S STRUCTURE OF PROCESS

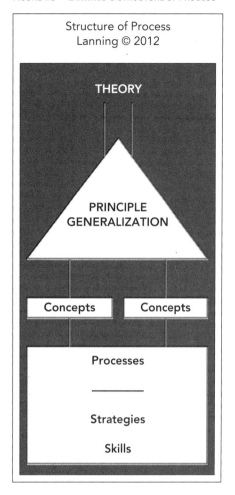

SOURCE: Lanning, L. A. (2013). *Designing a concept-based curriculum for English language arts: Meeting the Common Core with intellectual integrity, K-12.* Thousand Oaks, CA: Corwin.

Synergistic Thinking

So far in this chapter we have emphasized conceptual relationships, as they relate to both knowledge and processes, as the most important components of a good curriculum. While traditional curricula emphasize facts, topics, and isolated skills, we assert that in order to make these types of knowledge meaningful and transferrable, we must push students to engage with the upper levels of the Structure of Knowledge and Structure of Process.

However, we want to emphasize that this does *not* mean that facts, topics, and skills are unimportant. In fact, the dichotomy between teaching facts and skills or teaching big ideas and concepts is a false one. Students must use facts to discover conceptual relationships. And once they do that, they should use additional facts to deepen their

The dichotomy between teaching facts and skills or teaching big ideas and concepts is a false one. Students must use facts to discover conceptual relationships.

conceptual understanding. It is the strategic interplay between the lower level and conceptual levels of thinking that we're aiming for.

Consider the sets of facts and the corresponding concepts in Figure 1.9. Ask yourself this: How do the concepts help organize and illuminate the meaning of the facts? How do the facts encourage deeper, more nuanced understanding of the concepts?

FIGURE 1.9   SAMPLE TOPICS, FACTS, AND CONCEPTS

Course	Topic	Facts/Examples	Concepts
Geometry	Triangles	Side-side-side theorem Side-angle-side theorem	Proportionality Similarity
Chemistry	Acids and bases	pH scale Equilibrium constants (Ka, Kb) Strong acid/base Weak acid/base	Systems Equilibrium Disassociation Neutralization
Music	Classical period music	Mozart's Symphony No. 40 Beethoven's Piano Sonata No. 14	Time Rhythm Melody
Health and Physical Fitness	Basketball	Dribbling Layup Jump shot	Offensive versus defensive movement Systems
English Language Arts	Shakespeare	*Macbeth* King Duncan *Hamlet* Act II, Scene ii	Character Tragedy Text structure
Spanish	Subjunctive tense	Specific verb conjugation charts Ir Venir	Time Emphasis Verb aspect
Geography	Migration patterns	African diaspora Mexican immigration to the United States	Migration Conflict Choice Resource scarcity
Government	Electoral College	Winner-take-all Swing states *Bush v. Gore*	Proportionality Representation Democracy

Since most curriculum documents emphasize topics and facts, omitting the larger concepts at play, they trap teachers and students in the lower levels of learning. For instance, in a traditional Government unit on the Electoral College (outlined in Figure 1.9), students would likely be expected to memorize terms like "winner-take-all" and to explain the significance of the case *Bush v. Gore.* They would only be processing information at the factual level.

However, Concept-Based units demand that students process information on the factual level *while also* discerning larger patterns and coming to deeper transferable understandings about conceptual relationships. By emphasizing the relationships among concepts as discovered through facts and examples, teachers can encourage the interaction between the factual and conceptual levels of thinking. This interaction is what Erickson (2008) called *synergistic thinking,* and it is essential for deep, lasting learning.

Because synergistic thinking is the heart of conceptual learning, it must also be the heart of Concept-Based planning. Teachers, too, must learn to process their content on both the factual and conceptual levels. They must make personal meaning of the content by thinking through conceptual relationships for themselves. This is one of the biggest challenges of conceptual teaching—the intellectual demand is far greater than that of simply plotting out textbook chapters on a calendar. However, synergistic thinking is also what makes teaching for conceptual understanding more personally satisfying and enriching than teaching through a coverage model.

Unit Planning

So how do teachers use all of these insights—the Structure of Knowledge, the Structure of Process—to design Concept-Based units of study for their classrooms? Erickson et al. (2017) offered some useful tools for this process. They noted that, although there are many possible ways to write a unit plan, most good plans involve the following elements:

- A unit title
- A conceptual lens, concepts, and subconcepts
- A unit web
- Generalizations that put the concepts into relationships with one another
- Guiding questions
- Critical content and key skills that students will need to master
- Learning experiences and lessons
- Assessments: performance tasks and corresponding scoring guides

In a Concept-Based unit, all the parts work together to form a cohesive whole: Students tackle the guiding questions by investigating the critical content using key skills. For instance, science students tackle the question "*What happens when an ecosystem is disturbed?*" by investigating a few terrestrial ecosystems—tropical rain forests, deserts, and coniferous forests—using the key skill of testing hypotheses. Through their pursuit of the guiding question, students are looking at ecosystems through the conceptual lens of *interdependence* and employing the additional concepts of *change* and *adaptation,* and subconcepts specific to biology, such as *ecological succession* and *cyclical disturbance.* They ultimately come to understand that *when an ecosystem experiences a disturbance, new conditions enable the success of some species while disadvantaging others,* which they use to predict the impact of an underwater earthquake on an ocean ecosystem.

Erickson and Lanning identified 11 distinct steps of the Concept-Based unit planning process, as outlined in Figure 1.10.

We want to emphasize one key point about Concept-Based unit planning: It is hard work! The complex interplay among content, questions, concepts, and skills in a Concept-Based unit makes planning tough. Teachers often struggle to write their own statements of conceptual relationship and to craft conceptual questions. Instead of growing frustrated, though, we hope that Concept-Based teachers draw energy from the challenge of synergistic thinking. Think about the unit planning process this way: You are taking yourself on this intellectual journey so you can later play "tour guide" to students traveling along the same intellectual path.

Common Unit Planning Challenges

How do I think of and select concepts for my course?

- Start with the *bottom* of the Structure of Knowledge: topics and facts. Most teachers are given some direction regarding these components of the curriculum. Perhaps your state has content standards that indicate the major topics of study and factual content students should learn. Maybe you are expected to "cover" a certain set of textbook chapters or list of competencies. Begin here. Use the Structure of Knowledge diagram as a graphic organizer, working your way up.

- The concepts should be inherent in the content of your course and the ways of thinking that are important in your field. If you're having trouble "seeing" the concepts in your unit, start by learning more about the topics you need to teach. Keep asking yourself these questions: Why do kids need to learn this? Why are these topics important? What makes these facts or examples significant? What is the "story" here? What are the larger lessons at play?

- It may help to spiral concepts throughout your course. Bring concepts back up during the year to increase the sophistication of students' understanding. Just be sure that the microconcepts and factual content of later units serve to challenge, deepen, and expand upon understandings derived earlier in the year.

FIGURE 1.10   UNIT PLANNING STEPS

Step 1: Create a unit title.

The unit title can be engaging for students but needs to clearly indicate the content focus.

Step 2: Identify the conceptual lens.

The conceptual lens is a concept that provides focus and depth to the study and ensures synergistic thinking.

Step 3: Identify the unit strands.

Strands will be subject areas for inter-disciplinary units. The strands will be major headings, which break the unit title into manageable parts for intra-disciplinary units. In a process discipline, the strands are defined: understanding, responding, critiquing, and producing. Strands are placed in a web around the unit title.

Step 4: Web out the unit's topics and concepts under the strands.

After brainstorming, underline the concepts under each strand so they can be easily accessed in the next step.

Step 5: Write the generalizations you expect students to derive from the unit study.

Craft one or two generalizations using the conceptual lens, and one or two generalizations for each of the strands. Sometimes a generalization will address one or more strands (especially in a process discipline). A unit of study may have 5–9 generalizations depending on the grade level and length.

Step 6: Brainstorm the guiding questions.

Guiding questions facilitate student thinking toward the generalizations. Guiding questions should be coded as to type (factual, conceptual, debatable). Each generalization needs a mixed set of 3–5 factual and conceptual questions developed during the planning process, and 2 or 3 provocative questions for the unit as a whole.

Step 7: Identify the critical content.

The critical content is the factual knowledge required for grounding the generalizations, deepening knowledge of the unit topic, and defining what students may need to know about processes/skills.

Step 8: Identify the key skills.

The key skills may be drawn verbatim from academic standards or national curricula. Key skills transfer across applications and are not tied to specific topics until they appear in the learning experiences.

Step 9: Write the common, culminating assessment and scoring guide/rubric.

The culminating assessment reveals student understanding of an important generalization (or two), their knowledge of critical content, and key skills. Develop a scoring guide, or rubric, with specific criteria for evaluating student work on the task.

Step 10: Design suggested learning experiences.

Learning experiences ensure students are prepared for the expectations of the culminating assessment and reflect what students should understand, know, and be able to do by the end of the unit. Learning experiences are meaningful and authentic. Included in this section are suggestions for pacing, other assessments, differentiation strategies, and unit resources.

Step 11: Write the unit overview.

The unit overview is written to read to the students to hook or grab their interest and attention and to introduce them to the study.

SOURCE: Erickson, Lanning, & French. (2017). *Concept-Based curriculum and instruction for the thinking classroom* (2nd ed.). Thousand Oaks, CA: Corwin.

- Start big by asking yourself to write one or two sentences that summarize the "story" of your course. What is the one big lesson students should walk away with?
  - Algebra: In this course we learn to leverage known relationships among quantities to find what we don't know.
  - World History: This course is about how empires rise and fall.
  - Biology: This course shows students that all life is interconnected and interdependent.
  - Eighth-grade English: Finding the right words to express yourself can set you free.

What makes a good statement?

- It needs to be significant. If it feels really obvious or simple, it's not done, unless it's something that students often misunderstand or struggle to grasp.
- It needs to be appropriately challenging.
- It needs to be transferable. We need to think of multiple situations in which it holds true.

How do I make my statements better?

- Make sure the statement contains two or more concepts.
- Make sure it is not a skill or something the students will do. Stick to statements that complete this sentence: "Students will understand THAT . . ."
- Avoid weak verbs: is, are, have, affect, influence, impact (Erickson, 2008).
- Ask yourself this: Is this a developmentally appropriate yet sophisticated idea?
- Take the time to think deeply about these statements and to refine them. Put them away for a few hours or a few days and then come back. Make them more specific by asking yourself this: How? Why? Work on clarity, precision, and accuracy. Pay particular attention to the verbs, making sure they are as active and descriptive as possible (Erickson, 2008).
- Learn more! This is the trickiest part of planning a Concept-Based unit. But it is also the most rewarding. Rather than take the topics and facts at face value, you must push yourself to understand them deeply. You may need to do some new learning to uncover the deeper meaning inherent in the content. The harder you work on these generalizations, the more you discuss them with colleagues and test them by reading more widely in your field, the more precious and satisfying they become. And rightfully so—you're constructing knowledge!

Examine the sample statements of conceptual relationship in Figure 1.11. For practice, cover up the column marked "Better Statements" and focus only on the side marked "Weak Statements." Use some of the tips and questions here to improve the weak statements. Then challenge yourself: Can you improve upon the "Better Statements"?

FIGURE 1.11   SAMPLE STATEMENTS OF CONCEPTUAL RELATIONSHIP

Weak Statements	Better Statements
Students will understand the persuasive features advertisers use.	Students will understand that advertisers use persuasive features such as catchy slogans, captivating images, and simple but attractive logos to hook consumers.
Students will understand the relationships among formulas, values, quantities, measurement, and unknowns.	Students will understand that formulas demonstrate the relationship between several quantities. Formulas help us calculate a quantity when all of the values are given or can be easily measured. At the same time, when values are not given or not easily measured, we can use the formula in a different way to find the unknown quantity or quantities.
Students will understand that some processes are part of systems and they can create or destroy.	Students will understand that systems consist of interrelated parts—changes to one part of the system often lead to dramatic impacts on other parts of the system.

How many statements of conceptual relationships are ideal per unit?

- A good rule of thumb is five to nine statements per unit, depending on the unit length and the grade level (Erickson et al., 2017).

How do I write good questions?

- Strive for a balance of factual and conceptual questions that will ensure adequate engagement with both the lower level and conceptual level of learning. Include debatable questions to increase student interest and motivate thinking.

- Conceptual questions should ask about the nature of the *relationship* between concepts. The following question stems might be helpful in getting started. Remember that the blank spaces should be filled in with *concepts,* not facts or topics.

  - *What is the relationship between _____ and _____?*
  - *How does _____ impact _____?*
  - *What effect do _____ and _____ have on _____?*
  - *How do the forces of _____ and _____ interact?*

- Questions should guide students but not be too leading—this is a tough balance. A question should allow students to come up with the answer on their own through illustrative examples. This means that some of the weak verbs that we try to avoid when crafting generalizations—is, are, have, affect, influence, impact—are appropriate for questions because they leave the question open to many possible answers and approaches. For instance, the question "*Why do changes to the environment force living organisms to adapt?*" is much less open-ended than the alternative, "*How do environmental changes impact the organisms in an ecosystem?*" The first question provides a relationship—*changes to the environment force living organisms to adapt*—without demanding that students uncover it for themselves. Don't rob students of the opportunity to think for themselves.

- Questions can make or break a unit, so take the time to brainstorm and then narrow your questions down. For instance, we might begin with the question "What is the relationship between migration and conflict?" but then refocus it to allow students to attack just one aspect of this relationship: "Does migration inevitably lead to conflict?" There are pros and cons to both narrow and broad conceptual questions. In this case, the narrower question encourages kids to take a side and reconsider their position at various points in the unit without needing much modeling from the teacher. The larger "What is the relationship . . ." question allows for more variety and expansive thinking, but students would likely need more coaching in how to approach it.

Consider the three sets of sample questions in Figure 1.12. What type of thinking does each question encourage in students? Which questions best guide students toward understanding the relationship between two or more concepts? How do the questions in each set work together to guide students to a larger understanding?

FIGURE 1.12   SAMPLE CONCEPTUAL QUESTIONS

- What persuasive features do advertisers use?
- How and why do advertisers use persuasive features?
- What is the relationship between the persuasive features advertisers use and customers?

- What are formulas? Why do we use them?
- How do formulas help us when values are unknown or not easily measured?
- What is the relationship between formulas and unknown quantities?

- How does changing one part of a system impact other parts of the system?
- What happens if one part of a system changes?
- What is the relationship between the parts of a system and change?

Conclusion

We hope this chapter was a helpful review of the most important principles of Concept-Based Curriculum and of the basic steps for planning a Concept-Based unit. What excites us most about this curriculum model is its ability to awaken the potential of young people as intellectuals and as solvers of complex problems. When we envision the type of education that moves beyond rote learning and instead treats students as capable contributors to our global community, Concept-Based Curriculum is at the heart of it. This is because conceptual learning focuses on transferring deep, lasting insights to novel situations instead of "covering" a pile of information or set of discrete learning objectives. It encourages students to uncover meaningful truths and make use of them instead of cramming for tests that have no value beyond the schoolhouse walls.

By no means has this been a comprehensive guide. If you're left yearning for more in-depth explanations and further examples, we recommend that teachers of language (including world or foreign languages) and arts (music, drama, etc.) read Lanning's (2013) *Designing a Concept-Based Curriculum for English Language Arts: Meeting the Common Core With Intellectual Integrity, K-12* and mathematics teachers read Wathall's (2016) *Concept-Based Mathematics: Teaching for Deep Understanding in Secondary Classrooms*. Everyone else should check out Erickson et al.'s (2017) *Concept-Based Curriculum and Instruction for the Thinking Classroom*.

Chapter Review

- What role do facts, topics, and concepts play in a Concept-Based Curriculum? What about skills, strategies, and processes? Why are all of these elements important?

- What does it mean to make *transfer* the goal of learning? Why are concepts essential to the transfer of understanding from one situation to another?

- What are the greatest challenges of planning a Concept-Based unit? Which insights from this chapter might help you get "unstuck" during the tough parts of your planning process?

....

CHAPTER 2

How Do We Establish a Culture of Deep Learning?

In this chapter, we outline the importance of establishing a culture conducive to deep learning and offer strategies to help teachers—and students—move from coverage-based to Concept-Based Instruction. Getting started can be the toughest part. We recommend beginning with the following foundational principles of Concept-Based Instruction:

> "Learning about this way of teaching makes me wish I was 19 years old and could start my career all over again."
> —Neville Kirton, veteran teacher and department head

1. Conceptual learning happens best in a student-centered, **thinking–centered** classroom.
2. Students need to be **taught how** to learn conceptually.
3. Conceptual learning is **iterative;** students need chances to refine and increase the sophistication of their thinking.

This chapter offers a brief explanation of each of these principles and several illustrative instructional strategies to get you thinking—and teaching—like a Concept-Based teacher.

Setting the Foundation for a Thinking Classroom

Here's something every teacher knows: Initial student responses to academic prompts tend to be shallow, simple, and vague. It takes work and practice to make them deep, detailed, and profound. Students need to be aware of this tendency and the problems associated with it: forgetting most things learned, lacking quality of thought, and being unable to transfer learning to unfamiliar situations (to name a few).

We need to be explicit from the start that the goal of instruction is *depth* of learning and *quality* of thought that organizes and transfers to new situations. It's not the notion of "Yep, got it, let's move on" that characterizes most coverage-centered classrooms. This habit takes time to unlearn for both teacher and student.

The Foundation for Critical Thinking (Paul & Elder, 2008) points out that human thought is naturally partial and biased. It takes practice to make it better. Students enter schools with preconceptions about ideas and topics that are usually simple, disconnected, and sometimes incorrect. These ideas tend to be *unconscious*. It's our job to help young people unearth them and improve them.

This important truth has several implications for teaching for conceptual understanding. The first is that students' understanding of conceptual relationships inevitably builds from their preconceptions about the concepts. Especially when our goal is to engage students through universal concepts like change, systems, interdependence, or freedom, we must begin instruction by helping students become aware of their initial understanding of how these forces "work" in the world around them so they can consciously improve their understanding by making it more clear, precise, accurate, and sophisticated.

A second implication is that we must make it clear to students and ourselves that the goal is *growth*. Students often think of learning as binary: Either I know something or I don't. This is because so much of their school experience is geared toward acquiring discrete pieces of factual knowledge—spelling and vocabulary tests, grammar drills, and mad-minute math quizzes all reinforce for kids what it feels like to "know" something as opposed to "not knowing." Developing conceptual understanding works differently. It is not as easy for students to tell when they've "got it." Lessons where students compare their understanding before and after and showing models of student work that increase in sophistication will help them reorient their expectations of what learning feels like.

A third implication is that the learning environment must be one in which students feel comfortable exposing their own misunderstandings, changing their minds, and taking intellectual risks. The real work of conceptual learning involves admitting ignorance and seeking out one's own naivety, of making guesses and then rigorously testing them. An open, safe, supportive learning environment is essential.

> **We must take the time to reorient student expectations of and approaches to learning.**

This means that before we can successfully implement Concept-Based units and lessons, we must take the time to reorient student expectations of and approaches to learning. The following routines and strategies can be used to set the foundation for intellectual growth.

Strategy #1: Growth Mindset

Tell students that an enormous amount of research proves that intelligence is not something innate but rather about the amount of effort we put to learning and improving (Dweck, 2007). Show Figure 2.1 to students and ask them to discuss the difference in pairs.

FIGURE 2.1   FIXED VERSUS GROWTH MINDSET

Fixed Mindset	Growth Mindset
People with a fixed mindset believe they are either born smart or not, that they are either good at something or not. They emphasize raw talent over effort and do not like to work hard at things. If something doesn't come easily, they give up. These people do not understand the value of practice and unfortunately are easily frustrated. They do not like to receive feedback as they feel it threatens their intelligence.	People with a growth mindset believe that they can achieve success at nearly anything through hard work and practice. They understand that mistakes help us to learn and grow. When they are learning something new, they know that it will likely be difficult at first but that with practice they will get better and better. They appreciate feedback from teachers, coaches, mentors, and fellow students because they know it will help them improve.

After students have discussed initial differences, lead the class through a discussion of the following questions:

- Which mindset do you think very successful people have? Why?

- What things can we do in class to help build a culture where mistakes and feedback are a normal part of our learning?

- What are some things you can say to yourself to promote a growth mindset? For example, if you don't understand something we are doing in class, what can you say to yourself? What can you do?

Strategy #2: Intellectual Journals

Require each student to keep a notebook that chronicles his or her intellectual journey through your course. You might explain how this will be different from keeping a binder full of notes or handouts:

You may have used notebooks or binders to organize your notes and materials before. Usually, this means that at the end of the year your notebook is like a minitextbook, where you have stored important facts, vocabulary words, or instruction sheets. In this class, your notebook will serve a different purpose. Think of it as a scrapbook of your thinking. Each day you will record your ideas and thoughts as they develop. As the year goes by, you will be able to look back over your work to see your own intellectual growth.

Using intellectual journals is easy and can be adapted to meet the needs of any class structure. The basic principle is that students should be writing down their ideas about the concepts at various points in the unit. As their ideas evolve, their journal entries should become clearer, more precise, and more complex.

To use intellectual notebooks on a daily basis, start each class period with a question. As students begin class, ask them to write continuously in response to the question of the day for five minutes and draw a line beneath their initial answer once time is up. Then ask them to repeat this procedure for the last five minutes of class to show how their thinking has changed as a result of their learning experiences.

Strategy #3: Partner Coaching

Most teachers have used a "think–pair–share" structure to encourage students to discuss their ideas with a partner. This variation moves beyond simple idea exchange, putting each student in the position to help his or her partner grow as a thinker.

First, pose a question and allow students time to think about their responses. For instance, you may put a conceptual question up on the board (*Is equality necessary for freedom to exist?* or *How do functions demonstrate a mathematical relationship?*) and give students five minutes to write freely about the topic.

Next, set a goal for student thinking. For instance, you may want student thinking to get clearer, for students to articulate exactly what they think in an understandable, concise way. Or you may want students to consider complications to their ideas. Share the goal with students and offer some questions that can help them refine their thinking in relation to your goal.

FIGURE 2.2   PARTNER COACHING PROTOCOL

Round 1	Round 2
Partner A explains her thinking	Partner B explains his thinking
Partner B asks questions to help develop Partner A's thoughts: <ul><li>Could you give another example to show what you mean?</li><li>Is there any evidence that might contradict this idea?</li><li>Why might someone disagree with what you're saying?</li><li>What are you most certain about? Least certain about?</li><li>What makes this complicated?</li></ul>	Partner A asks questions to help develop Partner B's thoughts: <ul><li>Could you give another example to show what you mean?</li><li>Is there any evidence that might contradict this idea?</li><li>Why might someone disagree with what you're saying?</li><li>What are you most certain about? Least certain about?</li><li>What makes this complicated?</li></ul>

Finally, set up student pairs to coach each other toward improved thinking (see Figure 2.2). Partner A should be allowed a few minutes to explain her answer, while Partner B listens. Then Partner B should coach Partner A by asking her questions to push her thinking about the topic. After time is up, the partners should switch roles. After both rounds are up, all students should revise their original thinking by rewriting their answers to the prompt.

Strategy #4: At First I Thought . . . but Then . . . so Now I Think . . .

This simple template, adapted from *Making Thinking Visible: How to Promote Engagement, Understanding, and Independence for All Learners* (Ritchhart, Church, & Morrison, 2011), helps students identify their preconceptions and become aware of the way their understanding is changing as a result of their learning experiences. We like putting this sentence framework up on the board at the end of class and asking students to share ways their thinking has changed. It is helpful to model the evolution of your own thinking as an example:

> *At first I thought that fate was the most powerful force in Oedipus's life, meaning that despite all Oedipus's efforts, his acts of free will could never alter his fate. But then Marco's comments made me change my mind. Marco pointed out that Oedipus decided by his own free will to kill the man who attacked him along the path (who turned out to be his father), and Oedipus could have made other choices in that moment. So now I think that Oedipus's free will was also a powerful force in his life. Oedipus's belief that he had conquered fate led him to make rash, foolish decisions, which ultimately led to his downfall.*

Doing this regularly encourages students to notice how they and their peers think and learn differently and helps them gain metacognitive awareness of how their thoughts are changing in light of new information and experiences. Instead of asking students to share their thoughts verbally, you might ask them to write their responses on sticky notes and place them on the board as they leave the room. You can then start the next class by reading the notes and commenting on the trends you see.

Additional Strategies: Use these to help maintain a classroom culture where students support one another to become better thinkers.

- Ask students to describe their ideal class environment. What could your peers say or do to encourage you to take risks and develop strong ideas? What could the teacher do? What should we avoid? Create a poster of behaviors and attitudes to strive for and a poster of behaviors and attitudes to avoid. Every few weeks, spend 10 minutes of class time reflecting on the extent to which the class is on track.

- Make time in class for students to set personal goals for their learning and intellectual development. This is not the same as setting goals for grades or exam scores. Rather, these are goals about the type of thinking or understanding students want to achieve. For instance, one student may want to strengthen her ability to use supporting evidence in her essays. Another may be curious about the role of women scientists in making advances in the field of physics. Ask students to write down their intellectual interests and goals. By reading them, you'll show that you care about students' individuality and that you consider them to be intellectual beings.

- Recognize students for their strong or improved thinking. This does not need to be elaborate or overly burdensome. Just pay attention to students' conversations and writing over the course of the week and jot down two or three specific examples of clear, accurate, precise, logical, or sophisticated thinking. Spend five minutes each Friday acknowledging these students and holding their work up as an example to others.

- Allow students to offer "shout-outs" to their peers for helping them understand an idea or achieve a goal. Use the simple framework, "*I'd like to acknowledge ____ for helping me understand ____.*"

Teaching Students to Learn Conceptually

Once we've built the foundation of a thinking classroom, we can begin to build a conceptual classroom. Conceptual learning is not always easy or natural for students. Sadly, the longer they've been in school the less they are used to (and, therefore, the less they are good at) abstracting big ideas from concrete examples and transferring them to completely new situations. Even though their brains are wired for this type of thinking, it is rarely the intentional focus of their schoolwork. We need to be explicit about how this type of learning might be different from what they are accustomed to doing, especially for older students who are used to a more topic-based, coverage-centered classroom.

Students also need time to think about the definition of a concept and how concepts are different from facts. They need time to practice evaluating and writing their own statements of conceptual relationship. After a few attempts, though, we've seen students shift not only their approach to learning but their drive. When learning isn't just about retelling what they heard from someone else but using their personal intellect to create their own understandings and unravel complex situations, it brings the joy back to learning for students. It is an investment of a few class periods, but it will pay off!

Consider the following classroom exercises as a way of helping students transition to conceptual learning.

Strategy #5: Contrasting Traditional Learning With Conceptual Learning

Ask students to consider the two panels of images in Figure 2.3. Both panels present metaphors for learning. In the first panel, traditional learning is likened to collecting pebbles on the beach, while in the second, conceptual learning is likened to chiseling a sculpture from a rough piece of marble.

FIGURE 2.3   TRADITIONAL LEARNING VERSUS CONCEPT-BASED LEARNING

SOURCE: Jimmy Conde, graphic artist.

In the traditional model of learning, students play a rather passive role, waiting for the teacher to point out the facts and ideas they should "collect" in their jars. The goal of this type of learning is for students to hold all the facts in their heads until the end of the year (or until the day of the test), at which point they dump out the ideas they have learned to prove they have retained them. This type of learning does not invite students to shape the ideas or construct their own meaning; rather, students' minds are seen as empty jars waiting to be filled with the ideas of others.

Contrast this with the Concept-Based learning process, where students begin not with empty vessels but rather with their own preexisting ideas symbolized by the mound of rough stone waiting to be sculpted. In conceptual learning, we begin with what we already know and work to refine our ideas through disciplined study. As we learn, our ideas become more sophisticated, clear, precise, complex, and accurate, just as the sculpture takes on more nuanced form with each chisel mark. In the end, the product of our learning is a profound, well thought out idea of our own construction (not a jar full of details the teacher has asked us to memorize).

We like this exercise because it strengthens students' ability to think symbolically and metaphorically and provides an easy touchstone for later reference: "*Remember we're sculpting masterpieces, not collecting pebbles.*" Here are the basic steps:

1. Assign students to work with a partner. One student should be "Partner A" and one should be "Partner B."

2. Ask student pairs to first describe each panel and then discuss the ways in which each panel might serve as a metaphor for learning. You might say something like this:

    Today we are going to think about the difference between traditional learning and conceptual learning. To begin with, let's consider these two panels of images. Each one offers a metaphor for what it is like to learn at school. Let's see if you can figure out how these panels relate to learning. If you are Partner A, raise your hand. Partner A: You are going to focus on the top panel. I would like you to study your panel silently for one minute. Notice as many details as you can; after one minute you will explain the top panel to your partner. Partner B, raise your hand. Partner B: While your partner studies the top panel, you will focus on the bottom panel. Notice as many details as you can; after one minute you will explain the bottom panel to your partner.

    This is essentially a think–pair–share strategy, which we like because it ensures that every student has a specific role in the discussion (as either Partner A or Partner B) and, therefore, must take responsibility for the thinking in the lesson. As students discuss, circulate to monitor their discussions and offer quick prompts to groups that finish prematurely, signaling to them that the goal is not to "finish" the conversation but rather to **sustain their thinking in order to deepen it.**

3. Call on students to describe each panel in detail. After students share their initial thoughts, probe for deeper thinking:
    *   The first panel compares the learning process to collecting pebbles in a jar, while the second compares the learning process to sculpting a masterpiece from a mound of rock. Have you ever experienced learning that relates to either of these metaphors? Let's share some examples.
    *   What role does the student play in the learning process in each panel? What role does the teacher play? What are the pros and cons to each model?
    *   In the first panel, the student begins with an empty jar. In the second panel, the student begins with a rough mound of rock. Why is this an important difference?

- What product does the student end up with in the first panel? In the second? Which type of learning seems more valuable?

4. Ask students to compare traditional learning with conceptual learning in writing. Have them open to a new page in their notebooks and divide it in half. On the top half, they should write a paragraph that describes traditional learning. On the bottom half, they should write a paragraph that shows how conceptual learning is different. We like to use the model from the Foundation for Critical Thinking (2008) for writing explanatory paragraphs: State, Elaborate, Exemplify, Illustrate (SEEI for short). The sentence stems in Figure 2.4 offer a strong model for students to use as they think through a concept or idea.

FIGURE 2.4   SEEI TEMPLATE

(State the idea clearly) *Traditional learning is all about . . .*

(Elaborate on the idea) *In other words, the goal of traditional learning is . . . During the learning process, students mainly . . . while teachers mainly . . . In the end, the product of student learning is . . .*

(Exemplify) *For example . . .*

(Illustrate with a metaphor or image) *It's like . . .*

(State the difference clearly) *On the other hand, conceptual learning is all about . . .*

(Elaborate on the idea) *In other words, the goal of conceptual learning is not ____ but rather . . . During the conceptual learning process, students . . . while teachers . . . In the end, the product of student learning is . . .*

(Exemplify) *For example . . .*

(Illustrate with a metaphor or image) *It's like . . .*

SOURCE: Adapted from Paul & Elder (2013).

Strategy #6: Building Common Concept-Based Language

Students do not come prewired with the ability to distinguish facts from concepts or with the understanding of how facts, concepts, and generalizations are related to each other. Therefore, it is worthwhile to spend a class period explaining the structure of knowledge and providing examples of the building blocks of conceptual learning. Be sure to use a topic and concepts that students are already familiar with—the goal is to learn about *conceptual language* in this exercise; we don't want them to be intimidated by concepts they've never heard before.

By the end of this exercise, students should be able to distinguish between facts and examples, topics, concepts, and generalizations about conceptual relationships. They should also come to see the difference between a strong and weak generalization and to understand what we mean by "transfer."

1. Ask students this: What makes someone an expert? How are experts able to hold so much knowledge in their heads? After students provide their initial thoughts, push them to think more deeply through a specific context:

   Consider a veterinarian. Veterinary doctors must have extensive knowledge of the anatomy of dozens of different species. They must know how hundreds of drugs impact different animals differently, and how these drugs interact with each other. They must learn a wide array of surgical techniques and be able to improvise on them in response to each individual case. How are they able to remember and use so much information?

   Students may come up with a variety of ideas: Veterinarians must read and study extensively; veterinarians learn basic science as undergraduates and then build up more sophisticated knowledge over time; veterinarians learn by applying what they know and learning from their mistakes; veterinarians learn by getting feedback from others in the field.

2. Show students a diagram of the Structure of Knowledge and say the following: *Many different factors go into developing expertise: time, experience, study. But the most important difference between an "expert" and a "novice" is how the expert organizes the knowledge in his or her brain.* Ask students to examine the Structure of Knowledge diagram and hypothesize with a partner: *Consider this diagram that shows the way experts organize their knowledge. What do you notice? Why would experts think this way?*

3. Teach students briefly about the components in the Structure of Knowledge using an example they already know and understand: The goal here is to establish a common understanding of what is meant by the term "fact," versus "topic," versus "concept," versus "generalization."

4. Give students a chance to practice telling the difference between facts and concepts: Ask them to sort discipline-specific terms into two piles: facts and concepts. Consider the following list for an English language arts classroom:

Facts/examples:	Concepts:
Macbeth	Change
Oedipus	Identity
Romeo	Freedom
Act II	Fate
	Free will

5. Introduce statements of conceptual relationships (generalizations or principles): Show them some examples and ask: What are they? How do they

help us organize information? How do they help us figure out new situations?

6. Ask students to improve statements of conceptual relationships: Show them a few with weak verbs and proper nouns and ask them to fix them. Show them that asking "how" or "why" often helps us to make them stronger (Erickson 2008).

For instance, an English teacher may put the following examples up on the board for students to discuss and improve. Notice that even when one aspect of a statement has been improved, there is always room for greater refinement.

Sample Statement	Focus of Improvement
Fate and free will are forces that act on Oedipus.	Avoiding proper nouns
Fate and free will are two important concepts in literature.	Avoiding weak verbs
Fate is a stronger force than free will.	Increasing precision by asking "why?" or "how?"
An individual's free will is constrained by forces outside his or her control, such as fate.	Avoiding passive voice
Fate often constrains a person's free will in visible and invisible ways.	Increasing significance by asking "so what?"
Fate often constrains a person's free will, which means that individuals do not bear total responsibility for their actions.	Debating the statement's validity by brainstorming examples that confirm, contradict, or complicate the statement

Model briefly for students how a strong generalization can be built going "up" the Structure of Knowledge. Discuss the criteria that make a strong generalization using the examples.

7. Introduce transfer: Show students new situations. Slides with compelling images and a quick story work quite well. Short scenarios typed out on strips of paper also follow a good format. Ask them which conceptual relationship best unlocks the new situation and discuss why or how.

8. End with reflection: Ask students to again articulate the difference between a concept and a fact. How is learning about a concept different from learning about a fact? What is the definition of and importance of conceptual relationships? How do we improve statements of conceptual relationships? What are some ways to discover conceptual relationships? How do they help us unlock unfamiliar situations?

Unleashing the Power of Iterative Learning

Most traditional learning is linear. Think about a set of standards or a textbook. The underlying assumption seems to be that students will move on from topic to topic, fact to fact, in a straightforward sequence. Students accumulate knowledge by moving from one standard or chapter to the next, checking each one off as they go. Although the topics and facts may be carefully ordered to create a logical, progressive path through the course, rarely is emphasis placed on the connections among topics, facts, and ideas.

Here's how a linear classroom works: Each day the teacher posts an objective or goal to be achieved during the lesson. Lesson activities are designed to allow students to meet the daily goal, and students are responsible for mastering a "chunk" of content or a specific skill each day. After two or three weeks, students take a test that covers each of the daily goals from the unit. For instance, a week in a health class might consist of the following (see Figure 2.5):

FIGURE 2.5 SAMPLE HEALTH UNIT (TRADITIONAL)

Unit: Drugs and Addiction

- Day 1: Students will explain the difference between street drugs and medicines.

- Day 2: Students will classify drugs as stimulants, depressants, opiates, or hallucinogens.

- Day 3: Students will analyze the impacts of stimulants, depressants, opiates, and hallucinogens on the human body.

- Day 4: Students will describe the symptoms of drug addiction and the steps of rehabilitation.

- Day 5: Students will create plans for staying drug free using the refusal techniques in Chapter 3.

Notice that while the daily lessons proceed in a logical order, the goal of each lesson is still discrete and self-contained. The most intuitive students may grasp a larger structure or trajectory for their learning, but for most students the content appears episodic, segmented, and partial. There is rarely time to go back to the content of previous lessons to revise or challenge one's thinking. Every lesson is a move forward with new content and new goals.

Conceptual learning is not linear; it's iterative. By this we mean that learning happens through repetitions of the inquiry process, giving students multiple chances to develop ideas and deepen their understanding relative to a single learning goal. Consider the unit outline in Figure 2.6:

FIGURE 2.6   SAMPLE HEALTH UNIT (CONCEPT BASED)

Unit: Self-determination and addiction in the context of drug use

Question: How do drugs and addiction impact self-determination?

Inquiry cycles:

- Context #1: Alcohol and alcoholism
- Context #2: Tobacco use and nicotine addiction
- Context #3: Oxycontin, heroin, and opiate addiction
- Context #4: Marijuana and other hallucinogens

Much of the content included in the Concept-Based unit is the same as that included in the traditional, linear unit. Both units will expose students to specific drugs and their impacts on the body. The difference is that the *goal* of learning each day in the Concept-Based unit is to deepen student understanding of the relationship among concepts. In this case, students are coming to understand the larger concept of self-determination—the process by which a person controls his or her own life—in relation to addiction. Self-determination is a concept that students will come back to again and again in health class as they study everything from peer pressure to nutrition, giving them many chances to make meaning of this concept for themselves. Students will investigate several contexts, but this learning is far from episodic or disconnected. The concepts and iterative cycle of inquiry lend coherence and purpose to the learning.

Moreover, each context increases in complexity over the previous context. In the case of this health unit, the second context regarding tobacco introduces greater complexity when students learn about the tobacco industry's efforts to increase the addictiveness of cigarettes to increase profits. In the third context, another element of complexity is added when students study the use of opiates as prescribed by doctors for pain management. The final context adds complexity when students investigate disagreements about whether hallucinogens are addictive.

Strategy #7: Linear Versus Iterative Learning Processes

It is important to help students understand that iterative learning is organized differently than linear learning. Many students expect and even enjoy "checklist" learning because it feels productive and concrete. They may feel frustrated by iterative learning at first because the learning goal can never be "checked" off the list. This activity helps students understand and come to appreciate the iterative learning process.

FIGURE 2.7 ITERATIVE VERSUS LINEAR LEARNING PROCESSES

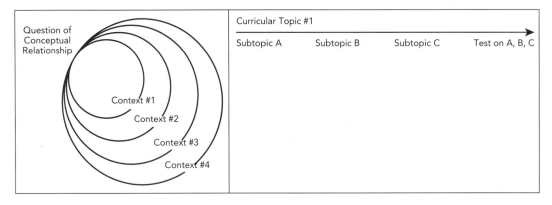

1. Display the two images in Figure 2.7 for the class and ask students to describe the differences they see. Together, list words that seem to describe each image. Here are a few key differences and observations to get you started:

Iterative Learning	Linear Learning
• Interlocking circles	• Straight line
• Moving in a repeated cycle	• Moving step-by-step
• Always returning to a conceptual question	• Always moving forward
• Distinct contexts united by concepts	• Broken down into subtopics
• Each context larger/more complicated than the previous one	• A leading to B; B leading to C

2. Present students with the following scenarios. Ask them which scenario relates most closely to the iterative process.

   Scenario A: Students are learning how to bake cakes. The teacher gives students the recipe for vanilla cake, students measure out and combine the ingredients, and then students bake the cake. The teacher tastes each cake to determine if students got it right.

   Scenario B: Students are learning how to bake cakes. First, students bake a vanilla cake using flour, sugar, eggs, baking powder, milk, and vanilla. They evaluate the taste and texture of the cake, noting its characteristics. Then students bake a second cake, this time adding butter, and again evaluate the taste and texture of their final product. Later, students bake a third cake using oil instead of butter, noting how this changes the cake. They continue to experiment with changes to the recipe until they have gotten the taste and texture just right.

3. Discuss the pros and cons of each type of learning. For instance, students may note that iterative learning promotes discovery through experimentation and

focuses on refining an idea or process. This gives students more agency in the learning process. They might worry, though, that learning this way will feel repetitive. They will likely note that linear learning is more straightforward but also less likely to produce learning that is deep or lasting.

We also suggest creating advance organizers using the iterative learning model shown in Figure 2.7. Consider constructing a simple handout with the specific conceptual question and separate contexts for your unit in this format. Or create a bulletin board display with the same visual depiction. This helps remind students where they are in the learning journey and how each context studied is meant to deepen their understanding of the relationship among concepts.

Strategy #8: Simple Versus Sophisticated, Static Versus Dynamic Ideas

Teaching through the iterative process described in this chapter only works if students know what it looks like to increase the sophistication of their thinking about the concepts. Many teachers get frustrated when student thinking remains stagnant and instruction seems only to reinforce shallow, superficial views of the concepts. *Why do we keep having the same discussion every single day, no matter the context we're studying?* The answer is simple: This is what kids expect from their learning experiences. School very often rewards kids for matching, not understanding, ideas.

Think about a group of ninth-grade students studying the concepts of power and exploitation in the context of apartheid in South Africa. They can define the concepts, recall examples, and recognize them in texts. *Aha! I spotted an example of exploitation! Aha! There's a reference to power over here!* It's a lot like "Where's Waldo?"—they know "exploitation" and "power" are the focus so they are scanning the context, using the concept as a device to screen out irrelevant information.

The problem is that all the "irrelevant" information is necessary to understanding how the concepts play out. This is the entire purpose of studying the concepts in several different contexts. What patterns do we notice in who exploits whom? When does exploitation tend to begin? What circumstances can we look out for to predict a rise or decline in exploitative practices?

If we want them to stop matching examples to concepts, and to actually deepen their understanding, we need to look at the gray areas surrounding the concepts, and kids need to be explicitly clued into this purpose. It seems obvious, but to kids it can be counterintuitive. They're on a "hunt and find" mission when they ought not to be.

Here is one way to help students understand the purpose of studying the concepts in various contexts through an iterative process.

1. Develop common definitions of the terms *simple, sophisticated, static,* and *dynamic.* Ask students to fold a piece of paper in half, and then in half again, to create four even boxes. Have them write the definition of one term in each box. Then, working with a partner, each student should list as many synonyms for each term as possible. The result might look something like this:

Simple: basic	Sophisticated: complex
• Uncomplicated	• Nuanced
• Naïve	• Informed, knowledgeable
• Unaware	• Consisting of many parts
• Easy, presenting no difficulty	• Difficult
• Straightforward	• Fully thought out
• Obvious	• Multifaceted
• Plain	
Static: remaining the same	**Dynamic: characterized by constant change or progress**
• Fixed	• Always improving
• Unchanging	• Growing
• Immobile	• Never settling
• Stuck	• Active
• Stable	

2. Present the two student portraits in Figure 2.8 and ask students which one seems to be developing a sophisticated, dynamic understanding.

3. When moving through each cycle of inquiry, students should look for ways the information can do each of the following:
   - **Confirm** their understanding
   - **Contradict** their understanding
   - **Qualify** their understanding
   - **Complicate** their understanding

4. Discuss what each of these terms means and might look like. Ask students these questions: *When did student B find information to confirm her understanding? Contradict it? Qualify or complicate it? What was the result? How did this make her ideas more sophisticated and dynamic?*

5. Introduce students to these phrases dealing with exceptions, nuances, and conditions. Ask students to brainstorm other phrases that might help them avoid overly simplistic thinking.
   - If . . . then . . .
   - Only when . . .

- But . . .
- Unless . . .
- If ___ had . . . then the result would change to . . .
- An exception to this is . . .

FIGURE 2.8   SIMPLE/STATIC IDEAS VERSUS SOPHISTICATED/DYNAMIC IDEAS

What is the relationship among change, environment, and interdependence?	
Student A:	**Student B:**
When there is a change in the environment, there is also a change in interdependent relationships.	*When there is a change in the environment, there is also a change in interdependent relationships.*
Inquiry Cycle #1: Ocean after an oil spill	
Students study the impacts of an oil spill in the Gulf Coast on the marine ecosystem. Students notice that some species of fish reacted to this oil spill by abandoning their old habitat, migrating to cleaner waters closer to the shore. Other species that relied on these fish as a food source, such as some birds, then migrated to follow the fish. Some did not, finding new sources of food.	
Student A:	**Student B:**
Yep! I was right! When the environment changed the interdependent relationships changed! Birds were no longer dependent on the fish.	*Hmm. I see. When there is a change in the environment, some interdependent relationships changed (birds found new sources of food), but some remained the same (birds maintained their food source by migrating with the fish).*
Inquiry Cycle #2: Killing of buffalo in the Great Plains	
Students study the impacts of mass killings of buffalo in the Great Plains of North America in the 19th century. They notice that many Native American tribes lived nomadic lifestyles, following the buffalo herds, until the buffalo population was decimated through overhunting. This overhunting was made possible by the introduction of the railroad into the environment. The decline in the buffalo population coincided with the confinement of Native Americans on reservations.	
Student A:	**Student B:**
Yep! I was right! When the environment changed the interdependent relationships changed! Native Americans were no longer dependent on the buffalo.	*I'm noticing that whenever humans introduce changes into an environment (oil spill, railroad), this change alters the relationships among species living in that environment, forcing each species to make adaptations.*

Conclusion

At the start of this chapter, we outlined three simple yet powerful principles for transitioning to a Concept-Based classroom:

1. Conceptual learning happens best in a student-centered, **thinking-centered** classroom.
2. Students need to be **taught how** to learn conceptually.
3. Conceptual learning is **iterative;** students need chances to refine and increase the sophistication of their thinking.

For many teachers, the biggest "Aha!" moment comes when they realize that Concept-Based classrooms operate differently than traditional coverage-based classrooms and that students need to be made aware of these differences. We have found that few teachers deliberately clue students in to the purpose of their learning or explain the intentionality behind the instructional activities planned. In secondary classrooms, where many teachers already struggle to fit their lessons into the constraints of a 50-minute class period, it can seem inefficient to take time out for such activities. But, as the old adage goes, it takes time to save time. Investing the time to build a thinking classroom where students know how to learn conceptually and come to expect the iterative learning process will pay dividends later.

Chapter Review

- What are the major differences between a traditional coverage-centered classroom and a Concept-Based classroom?
- What is the relationship between a growth mindset and conceptual learning?
- Why should we take the time to teach students how to learn conceptually? What frustrations might we experience if we don't do this?
- What new challenges are teachers likely to face as they transition to conceptual teaching? What strategies might help teachers overcome these challenges?
- How does thinking about Concept-Based learning as *iterative* help clarify your vision of what conceptual teaching looks like?

CHAPTER 3

What Are the Building Blocks of Concept-Based Instruction?

The previous chapter outlines our recommendations for teachers transitioning to a Concept-Based classroom. For instruction to work, teachers must first create a thinking-centered classroom where students expect iterative learning and understand that the goal is to develop sophisticated and transferable understandings.

Next, we turn our attention to the instructional principles that guide conceptual teachers in designing learning experiences for their students:

1. We need to expose students' **pre-instructional understanding** of the concepts and conceptual relationship.
2. A deep understanding of **each concept by itself** is necessary for a sophisticated understanding of the relationship among several concepts.
3. Students must **uncover** the conceptual relationship for themselves.
4. **Transfer** is both a means and an end of conceptual learning.

Starting With Students' Pre-Instructional Understandings

In their groundbreaking report for teachers, *How Students Learn: History, Mathematics, and Science in the Classroom,* Donovan and Bransford (2005) reminded us of a basic truth about learning:

> Students come to the classroom with preconceptions about how the world works. If their initial understanding is not engaged, they may fail to grasp the new concepts and information, or they may learn them

for purposes of a test but revert to their preconceptions outside the classroom. (p. 1)

This is especially important for conceptual teachers. Our ultimate goal is to develop deep and lasting understanding in our students so that they can use their learning to tackle big, messy, real-world challenges ranging from climate change to domestic violence. Research tells us that in order to reach this goal, we must first expose, and then deal directly with, the pre-instructional understandings students bring with them each day.

Another reason that starting with students' pre-instructional understandings is so important is that it allows us to track growth in students' understanding of the concepts and conceptual relationships at the heart of a unit of study. If we fail to make students' prior understanding visible early on, it is entirely possible that they coast through a lesson or entire unit without actually learning anything new. Without a record of students' initial thinking about the concepts, neither teacher nor student really knows the impact of a learning experience. Did students gain a deeper, clearer, more precise, or more sophisticated understanding of the concepts? Without a baseline, we have no way to tell.

Gauging students' pre-instructional understanding does not need to be fancy or take up much instructional time. Consider the usefulness of the following strategies.

Strategy #1: Individual Journaling

- Post a simple conceptual question, or series of questions, on the board for students to consider.
- Ask them to respond to the question(s) in their journals.

It is important that all students have time to think and write something substantive about the concepts before time is up, so be sure to monitor student responses and encourage reluctant writers. For an exercise like this, be intentional in the composition of your questions. It may be helpful to consider a variety of question types, such as those captured in Figure 3.1. Think about which questions would best spark student thought and elicit the understandings you are looking for.

After students have a chance to write, it is often helpful for them to make their understandings visible to each other:

- Ask students to share their responses with a partner, looking for similarities and differences in their ideas.
- Call on several students at random and ask them to share their ideas with the whole class. After each student shares, ask others to agree or disagree or to provide related examples.
- For debatable questions, take a quick poll to see the spread of opinions across the class.

FIGURE 3.1   SAMPLE CONCEPTUAL QUESTIONS

Defining Well-Known Concepts	Defining Lesser Known Concepts	Understanding Relationships	Debating Relationships
What is your definition of "freedom"? Give an example.	Have you ever heard the term "equity" before? What do you think this concept means?	How are freedom and equality related?	Which is more important for society to achieve: freedom or equality?
Is "no rules" a good definition for "freedom"? Why or why not? How would you define it?	Is it ever fair to treat people differently, or is it most fair to treat everyone the same? Explain your thinking.	What is the relationship between equality and equity? How are these concepts different? How are they similar?	Does freedom naturally produce inequalities?
			To achieve equality, is it necessary to give up some of our freedom?

Strategy #2: Four Corners

Another strategy for making student understanding visible to the entire class is a four corners activity. We love this one because it combines physical movement with the requirement that every student must respond to the question at hand.

The procedure is simple:

1. Post a conceptual question in multiple-choice format for students to consider. We like to start with the following stem: *Which of the following best matches your understanding of ____?* This works for gauging understanding of individual concepts as well as conceptual relationships. Here is an example: *Which of the following best matches your understanding of **metaphor**?*
   a. *A comparison between two things*
   b. *A figure of speech that matches one thing to another*
   c. *Making two things equal to each other*
   d. *A thing regarded as representative or symbolic of something else*

2. Give students a few minutes of silent thinking time. Set a timer, if only for yourself, and do not allow students to share their answers prematurely. It's important that all students have a chance to consider the question for themselves. Also, students who experience a "gut reaction" to the question will have time to reconsider as they think things through. We also find it useful to have students write down an answer during the silent thinking time, especially if we suspect that students might change their answers once they see where their peers are moving.

3. Assign each answer to a corner of the classroom. You may even want to post one answer in each corner using chart paper. Ask students to vote with their feet by moving to the corner of the answer they chose.

4. Have groups discuss the reasoning behind their choice and ask representatives of each group to share with the whole class. Or, to boost a low-energy class, have corner groups try to recruit members of the other groups by arguing the merits of their answer choice.

Strategy #3: Take a Stand, Then Divide and Slide

To tap further into teenagers' affinity for debate, consider posing a debatable question (one with two clear, opposing answers) or posting a statement with which students can agree or disagree.

After some thinking time, ask students to "take a stand" on the question and then "divide and slide" before debating their position. Here are the steps:

1. Give students a few minutes of silent thinking time to consider your debatable question or agree/disagree statement. For instance, the teacher may ask students the following:
   *Which is more important for society to achieve: **freedom** or **equality**?*

   or

   *Is it possible for a writer to remove his or her **bias** while writing?*

2. Ask students to take a stand on the question by physically lining up along a spectrum of answer choices. In the case of the question above, one end of the spectrum would be the answer choice "freedom" and the other end would be "equality." In the case of the second question, one end of the spectrum would be the answer choice "yes" and the other end "no." The desired result is one single file line, so it may help to ask students to line up against a wall or along a line of tape adhered to the floor. For older students, posting a visual on the board (like the one that follows) may suffice.

Freedom is most important   **Equality** is most important

Freedom and **equality** are equally important

3. Once students have formed a single file line along the "take a stand" spectrum, divide the line exactly in half and ask all students on one side to take a giant step away from the line. Students should still be in the same single file order, but now they form two separate lines, as with the following:

Next, have one half of the line "slide" toward the other half so students are standing in two parallel lines. Students should have a partner across from them in the opposite line whose views on the question are different from their own. The formation will look like this:

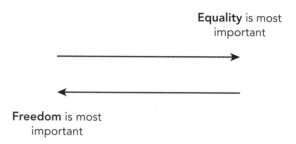

4. Finally, ask students to share their position on the question and reasoning behind it with the partner across from them in the opposite line. Or, to add some excitement, ask them to engage in a minidebate with their partner by giving each side one or two minutes to make the case for their position. Take the time to notice where students line up and to listen in on their discussions or debates to gauge the range of understandings in the class.

5. We always like to ask students to record their responses to the conceptual question in writing before moving on. The take a stand and divide and slide activity makes their thoughts visible for a short period of time, but it is important to have a written snapshot of their thinking to look back at later in the unit of study. Provide a few minutes of silent journaling time to wrap up the activity.

Strategy #4: Gallery Walk With Chalk Talk

Another way to get students up and moving while capturing their initial understanding of the concepts is to conduct a gallery walk activity that invites them to record their thinking and respond to others' thinking on poster paper around the room.

1. Set up several pieces of poster paper around the room, each with a separate conceptual question on it. Consider including a variety of questions, such as those in Figure 3.1, to elicit different types of thinking from students at each station. Students will be rotating around the room, writing out their answers

on each poster, so make sure there is plenty of blank space for student responses.

2.   Assign each student a poster as a starting place, with no more than three students at any given poster. For a large class, we like to make duplicate posters so that students can spread out and have space to write even if the questions on many of the posters are the same. More than three per poster is just too crowded. At their first poster, students should spend some time thinking about the question and then write a thoughtful answer before signing their name.

3.   At each subsequent poster, students should begin by reading what their peers have written and then respond. Encourage students to respond directly to one another, either by agreeing and adding on, disagreeing with a reason, or asking a question. The goal is to engage in a written conversation and explore ideas. You may want to post the following sentence starters to help keep them on track:
     •   *I agree with Maria and would like to add that . . .*
     •   *I disagree, Sean, because . . .*
     •   *Jasmine's comment makes me wonder . . .*

4.   Once students have made a full lap of the room, they should return to their original poster to read the responses that have accumulated during the activity. Ask one spokesperson per poster to share the most common, unique, or interesting ideas they find there.

One of the reasons we like the gallery walk with chalk talk is that it's the perfect bookend activity. At the end of the unit, put the posters back up and ask students to walk back through to find their original responses. Have them reply to themselves using sticky notes or a different color marker. Afterward, they can journal about how their thinking has changed over the course of their learning.

This brings us to an important point: Although we've listed these strategies as ways to engage students' prior understanding of concepts, the same activities can be used throughout a Concept-Based unit to gauge student progress. They are fun and interactive. Plus, once students have done them a few times, they can be executed quite efficiently, taking up no more than 15 minutes of instructional time.

Introducing New Concepts

The first five strategies in this chapter assume that the concepts you're dealing with are somewhat familiar to students. For instance, we've used the concepts of freedom, equality, metaphor, and bias as examples, which are common concepts that students are likely to know from previous contexts.

But in order to achieve depth of understanding and disciplinary competence, secondary students also need to learn new concepts with which they have had no prior encounters. For instance, math students must come to understand the concept of **trigonometric functions,** English students will need to learn the concept of **soliloquy,** and economics students should develop awareness of the concept of **opportunity cost.** Although it may be helpful to expose students' prior understandings of *related* concepts—the concept of **functions** before studying trigonometric functions, or the concept of **alternatives** before studying opportunity cost—most students will have little pre-instructional understanding of the discipline-specific concepts listed here.

When introducing a new concept, the biggest pitfall is treating it like a fact. Many teachers instinctively want to teach concepts like vocabulary words, offering textbook definitions and then quizzing kids on those definitions later. The problem here is that students, even at the secondary level, struggle to distinguish meaningfully between concepts and facts on their own. Left to their own devices, they'll dutifully go home and memorize definitions without really understanding much at all. Then they—and their teachers—will be disappointed when they can't apply or analyze or evaluate based on the concepts.

Helping students *understand* a concept means more than knowing a definition. Consider using the concept attainment and SEEI strategies that follow to encourage more than memorization.

Strategy #5: Concept Attainment

Concept attainment lessons are super easy to plan and kids love them because it feels like they're putting together the clues in a mystery. The following steps mimic the brain's natural concept-formation process by drawing out patterns from examples and nonexamples:

1. **Investigating examples:** The goal of a concept attainment lesson is for students to develop their own "definition" of a concept by investigating many examples. This works particularly well for discipline-specific concepts to which students won't have had a lot of previous exposure or for which their prior understanding is likely naive or incomplete. For instance:
   - **Science** students are studying physical and chemical changes in matter. To understand what is meant by "physical change," the teacher shows slides with several examples. The first might be an ice cube melting on the counter, then perhaps a lake freezing over in the winter. Students begin to form hypotheses: *Physical changes have to do with temperature,* or *physical changes happen when a substance moves between the liquid and solid states.* Then the teacher shows more examples: someone slicing a carrot, mixing a cake batter, shattering a window, crumpling up a piece of foil. Students revise their answer in light of the new examples, since none of these has to do with temperature or changes in state. Perhaps they notice that all the changes are visible to the naked eye. The teacher then

shows **nonexamples** to help students refine their definitions. Sometimes it helps to show examples and nonexamples in pairs. For instance, the teacher may juxtapose the example of chopping wood with the non-example of burning wood, or the example of mixing cake batter with the nonexample of baking a cake. The class continues this way with progressively more nuanced examples and nonexamples until students have formed specific criteria to help them accurately judge examples from nonexamples on their own.

- High school **history** students are studying "absolutism." They start by reading four short descriptions of absolute monarchs—King Philip II of Spain, France's Louis XIV, Russia's Peter the Great, Frederick III of Norway. Knowing that these are all *examples,* they look for common traits. They may notice that the first two monarchs are Catholic but, upon reading about Peter the Great, will reject this as a characteristic of "absolutism" because Peter was Russian Orthodox. But they might be savvy enough to notice that all of these monarchs claimed a divine right to rule.

What we *love* about this step is that usually history students would be reading about Philip II and Louis the XIV with the intention of highlighting and memorizing the dates of their reign and terms like "Edict of Nantes" or "Spanish Armada." But they are so much more engaged when we explain to them that their goal is *not* to find and memorize these terms, which are *facts,* but rather to use these facts to investigate the larger *concept.*

2. **Distinguishing examples from nonexamples:** After students have working definitions (usually lists of criteria) for the target concept, they practice applying these definitions to more examples and nonexamples.
   - The science teacher gives groups of students several photographs of physical changes mixed up with photographs of chemical changes (or other nonphysical changes). Using their definitions, students sort the photos into two piles: physical changes and nonphysical changes. Then they compare with a neighboring group to see if the result was the same.
   - The history teacher asks student pairs to research one from a list of other leaders to determine whether they fit the concept of absolutism: Benito Mussolini of Italy, the emperors of the Ming dynasty in China, William and Mary of England, King Salman of Saudi Arabia, for instance. Pairs share their findings with the class, using evidence to defend their claim that the leader they researched was or was not an example of absolutism.

3. **Confirming critical attributes:** Finally, the teacher guides students through the critical attributes of the concept. That's right, the more formal "definition" of the concept comes at the *end* of the lesson. By this time, students have a fairly solid understanding of the concept, so they actually *understand* what they're writing down and won't go home to try to *memorize* the definition like it's a fact.

4. **Reflecting:** It's also nice to spend a little time reflecting at the end of the lesson. When was it that you "got" the concept? Which examples or nonexamples were most challenging for you? How did your partner/group help you develop your understanding of the concept? What makes a concept different from a fact? How is it different to learn about a concept (as opposed to a fact)?

5. **Using a concept wall and concept maps:** It's a good idea to designate one space of the room as your concept wall—a space to put all the concepts as you study them. Students can use them to frequently draw concept maps and connections between and among different concepts at different points throughout the school year, as most concepts in every discipline are related to each other in some way.

Strategy #6: SEEI Presentations

You may remember this acronym from one of the exercises outlined in Chapter 2. It's one of our favorite tools from the Foundation for Critical Thinking and we highly recommend that you check out their miniguidebooks. This one can be found in *The Thinker's Guide to How to Write a Paragraph* (Paul & Elder, 2008). The last step of *illustrate* is especially good for building their conceptual muscle, as making a comparison in a metaphor inherently requires abstracting to the conceptual level. Using this strategy has the added impact of helping students develop strong literacy skills.

The strategy itself is incredibly simple: Give students written explanations of a key concept in all of its complexities, and then ask them to teach the concept to others. This is *not* the same as asking students to copy down a definition for the concept or briefly explain it to a partner. Notice how the following steps encourage more substantive engagement with the concept and produce greater understanding.

1. Begin by finding (or writing) a clear but complex explanation of the target concept. We find that most mathematics and science textbooks offer such explanations, as well as illustrative examples, but that teachers rarely assign them because they are difficult to understand. This activity works best when there is an element of challenge, so resist the urge to oversimplify the explanation. A one- or two-page overview with plenty of elaboration and some examples tends to work best. You could also use short video clips.

2. Assign students to small groups and ask them to read the explanation out loud together with the goal of understanding the target concept. Encourage them to ask questions and seek answers using the resources available to them (Internet, textbooks, the teacher, etc.).

3. Once students have a basic understanding of the concept, have them work together to explain the concept in their own words using the SEEI model (see Figure 3.2). Have them write out their explanation on poster paper or other means so it will be visible to others during their presentation.

FIGURE 3.2   SEEI MODEL

State, Elaborate, Exemplify, Illustrate (SEEI)
(State the idea clearly)
(Elaborate on the idea) *In other words . . . This is not to say . . . but rather . . .*
(Exemplify) *For example . . . However, a nonexample would be . . . because . . .*
(Illustrate with a metaphor or image) *It's like . . .*

SOURCE: Adapted from Paul & Elder (2013).

Encourage students to spend ample time crafting their explanation to make sure it is clear and precise. Circulate to provide feedback as they go. Encourage them to be creative and generate good examples, nonexamples, and illustrations of the concept. Disallow the use of examples embedded in the provided text. Students should come up with their own examples and nonexamples to demonstrate understanding.

4. Have student groups present to the class. You may ask a few groups to share their statements of the idea and others to elaborate on it or provide examples. We like to have all groups share their illustrations, since they tend to be more varied than the other elements of the explanation. In fact, the illustrations are often the best indicators of understanding (or misunderstanding), as students are required to make abstract comparisons or put their understanding into nonlinguistic form. Encourage the audience to ask questions to gauge the presenters' understanding and elucidate meaning.

Concept-Based Teaching in Two Words: Uncover and Transfer

The preceding strategies are important first steps in the journey for conceptual understanding. When dealing with familiar concepts, we must first gauge students' pre-instructional understandings. We must also be deliberate in how we introduce new concepts. But the crux of conceptual learning is developing deep, sophisticated understandings about conceptual *relationships*. The next chapter provides four lesson frameworks for this most important aspect of conceptual teaching, but the following two sections offer two related explanations to help frame the process of students in developing understandings about the conceptual relationships.

A few years ago, our colleague Dave Yarmchuk made some amazing stickers to help the Concept-Based model "stick" in teachers' brains. They were oh-so-simple, but oh-so-effective. We had read Erickson's and Lanning's books on Concept-Based Curriculum and Instruction and the supporting research from the National Research Council in *How Students Learn,* along with tons of discipline-specific books about the fundamental and powerful concepts that underpin mathematics, science, history, language arts, music, and other subjects. It was complex, but Yarmchuck managed to capture the essence of what we were finding in two little words:

Uncover → Transfer

In these two words, his stickers summed up the most important principles of conceptual learning and helped teachers avoid the two most common pitfalls.

Step #1: Uncover. If you're a fan of *Understanding by Design*, you will recognize the term *uncoverage* from Wiggins and McTighe (2005). Uncoverage means that instead of the teacher "covering" the content kids need to know—as in, "Jose, you should know this; we covered it on Friday"—he or she needs to plan for *students* to uncover the big ideas of the unit through inquiry.

The biggest pitfall we've seen teachers fall into with conceptual teaching is "covering" the concept by telling kids what the relationship between two concepts is. No joke, we've walked into classrooms where kids were copying notes from the board that said, *Some identity groups hold more power in society than others.* This is *not* what we mean when we say kids need to learn about the relationship between identity and power. The teacher may have "covered" identity, but the kids never "uncovered" its meaning, nor did they gain any insight into the way it shapes their world. Uncoverage is key.

Step #2: Transfer. Once students uncover or discover the relationship between two or more concepts, they can use this knowledge to unlock new situations. This is the goal of conceptual learning: transfer. For instance, students in a history class might study the women's rights movement of the 1840s to uncover the idea that, "*The complexity of multiple group identities can prevent groups from uniting behind a common cause.*" This insight is a beautiful product in itself, and many teachers fall into the trap of stopping here. We've made it! Success! But understanding the relationship among concepts is just step one. The real reason we want students to uncover these relationships is so they begin to see their world differently. We want them to discover conceptual relationships so they can use their new knowledge to analyze problems, make decisions, and influence others in ways that matter to them.

After students have uncovered a relationship, they need to practice transfer. Consider this next step: Students read articles, watch videos, or conduct interviews related to the recent effort for marriage equality or the BlackLivesMatter movement. The teacher asks this: "*Knowing what you do about identity, unity, and power, how might you design an ad campaign that brings new supporters to these movements?*" Students then work in groups to come up with ad campaigns that take into consideration the complexity of multiple group identities, present them to the class, and discuss how their understanding of identity, power, and unity helped influence their choices. Does this take more time? Will you cover less content? Yes, of course! Conceptual learning demands time and energy for transfer. It's not optional!

> Once students uncover or discover the relationship between two or more concepts, they can use this knowledge to unlock new situations.

Here's the tricky part about transfer: It's easy to get sucked into topical extensions rather than conceptual transfer. Topical extensions might mean teaching a unit on the 19th-century women's rights movement and then asking students to evaluate how many of the goals of that movement have actually been achieved today. In this case, students use their knowledge of the topic studied, and the facts, but they don't actually have to use the concepts at all. It's a lovely extension activity. It probably boosts engagement. It helps kids see "real-world connections." But it's not conceptual transfer because you're not asking them to apply insights about the concepts.

As students practice transfer to new situations, they can also practice research skills by finding their own new contexts. To keep with the same example above about the 19th-century women's movement, a unit that reaches the conceptual level with concepts such as *movements, change,* and *power* would uncover a relationship among them, such as the following: *Movements for change inevitably challenge the existing power structure.* An authentic transfer task would ask students to find a current example and prove that this idea holds true, using evidence from both the women's movement studied in class and the current example found through research.

Also notice that a transfer task makes a meaningful performance assessment for conceptual understanding. There's no way for students to succeed in this task by simply memorizing something the teacher said in class. You'll see right away if they don't understand the concepts or if their ability to apply them is weak. When you give them something new and ask them to show you how their understanding of the concepts helps them problem solve, there's no faking. They'll know it, and you'll know it.

Strategy #7: Learning as Uncovering and Transferring Understanding

Show the image in Figure 3.3 to students and discuss the following questions:

FIGURE 3.3 UNCOVER AND TRANSFER

SOURCE: Jimmy Conde, graphic artist.

- What do the keys represent in a Concept-Based classroom? *The conceptual relationships.*

- Why are they buried underground? *Because the students must uncover them through specific contexts.*

- What does the treasure chest represent? *A new or novel situation they can unlock with their conceptual understanding.*

- Where does the burden of thinking rely? *On the learner and not the teacher.*

The best part about these two principles—uncover and transfer—is that they put the burden of thinking on the student. This is key for maximizing learning.

Uncover: The Conceptual Inquiry Cycle

Now that we understand the process of uncover and transfer, let's contrast this type of learning against traditional, linear learning. Again, the most important point to remember for conceptual learning is that students **uncover** the conceptual relationships and express their unique understanding of this relationship in their own words. That is why the guiding questions and the art of crafting them are so important. This way of teaching is typically called inquiry-based, inductive, or constructivist teaching. It is the best method for deep understanding because the students make meaning for themselves.

Strategy #8: The Conceptual Inquiry Cycle

At a very basic level, instruction should cycle frequently through two major components (see Figure 3.4):

- Students respond to abstract questions of conceptual relationship.
- Students explore a specific context—a mathematical problem, scientific experiment, historical moment, or passage of text—in which the concepts play a major role.

The following steps explain the basic process of teaching for deep, conceptual understanding:

FIGURE 3.4   CONCEPTUAL INQUIRY CYCLE

1. Pose a conceptual question to students and then take them through a specific context that illustrates the relationship. In other words, the context helps to answer the abstract conceptual question.

2. After careful study of the specific context, students reconsider the conceptual question in light of the information studied. Specific contexts provide the foundation for understanding

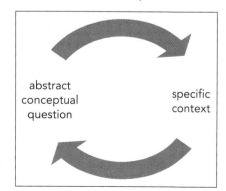

abstract conceptual question

specific context

the more abstract conceptual relationship, and the concepts help students gain insight into the specific contexts studied. **The facts and examples studied in the new context become the evidence to support their generalization about the concepts.** Students must provide **evidence** to illustrate the statements of conceptual relationship; this is essential.

3. The next step is to provide a second context to further illustrate the relationship between the concepts. The more contexts or facts they collect, the deeper their understanding and the more sophisticated their ability is to apply it to new situations. By studying the same conceptual question in many different contexts, we are able to balance depth of learning with breadth of learning. The breadth comes from the variety of contexts and examples to which students are exposed. However, unlike coverage-centered classrooms, the Concept-Based classroom also achieves a depth of understanding by filtering the many contexts through the concepts of the unit.

What does this look like in a classroom? Consider the following high school biology example.

Students study the relationship between external and internal environments of organisms in a broad range of contexts. As shown in Figure 3.5, they may begin with the simplest or clearest example and move on to progressively more complex examples to deepen and complicate their understanding as the unit goes on. In the end, they have gained knowledge of excretory systems among animals and of the human digestive, circulatory, and nervous systems. More importantly, though, they have used their study of these topics to uncover a deep, enduring understanding about ways in which external environments impact the internal environments of living organisms. This is much more interesting and useful to students than a unit that "covers" all of these systems but does not bring conceptual coherence to the learning.

FIGURE 3.5   DEEPER LEARNING IN BIOLOGY (BY IBIS NIÑO LOPEZ AND CLARA GARAVITO)

Real classroom example: Biology

Conceptual question: What is the relationship between the external and internal environment of organisms?

Contexts:

- Introductory context: Salmon moving from saltwater to freshwater and the excretory system
- Comparing the excretory system among animals living in different habitats
- The human digestive system
- The human circulatory system
- The human nervous system

In a nutshell, **we first pose an interesting question about the nature of a conceptual relationship for students to answer.** This allows the students and the teacher to become aware of any preconceptions, prior knowledge, and misunderstandings. Then, **students explore the concepts in a specific context (a factual example, text, or other slice of content) that allows them to back up to answer the question.** The context is chosen carefully to enable discovery of the answer to the conceptual question. The students' responses to the conceptual question in light of the facts of the specific context serve as the evidence of understanding (or not) and are the most important part.

The introductory context needs more direction and guidance from the teacher. Early on, the teacher may provide guiding questions to lead students to a specific insight or present the context in a way that highlights the concepts at play. Texts, videos, or class activities should be designed to lead students down a fairly straightforward path of understanding. The goal is convergent, meaning that the teacher wants all students to uncover (roughly) the same conceptual relationship here.

As students deepen their understanding by applying it to new contexts, their need for these teacher supports diminishes. Now, instead of pushing students toward a certain understanding of the conceptual relationship, the teacher begins to challenge and complicate the understandings that students are coming to. At this point the goal can be divergent, meaning that students can uncover unique conceptual relationships, perhaps even arriving at conclusions that contradict those of their peers for extremely deep learning. Of course, all generalizations must be accompanied by strong evidence from the contexts.

You may notice that the conceptual inquiry process is iterative. By this we mean that students should study the same conceptual relationship as it appears in several different contexts. In an English classroom, this might mean that students return to the conceptual question after reading each act of *Romeo and Juliet,* with each section of the play serving as a separate context. Another option would be to pair *Romeo and Juliet* with *Oedipus Rex,* studying the same concepts in the context of two different plays. In a mathematics classroom these contexts may be a series of problems that escalate in complexity. In any case, **it is essential that students stop to explicitly reconsider their understanding of the conceptual relationship by returning to the conceptual question several times throughout the unit of study, not just at the end.**

This brings us to an essential part of uncovering the relationship among the concepts: refining and increasing the sophistication of students' ideas. Remember that we always begin with students' preconceptions about the concepts. Oftentimes, students already know quite a bit about the concepts from their prior learning and personal experience. It is not enough for students to go through the motions of the unit, allowing their ideas to remain static. Students must show their learning by tracing the evolution of their thinking as they make their ideas clearer, more precise, more logical, and more sophisticated. This is another key component for achieving deeper learning.

Strategy #9: Comparing Surface and Deep Learning

As students move through the conceptual inquiry cycle, be sure to remind them of the process and goal of iterative learning. Consider showing them the visual in Figure 3.6 and ask them to compare the two swimmers. What are the implications? Students should come up with ideas such as, the deeper the diver goes, the more interesting the ocean becomes. If we only stay at the surface, learning can be quite boring. Each new context students study should take them deeper, helping their generalizations become more interesting, insightful, and well-supported.

FIGURE 3.6   SURFACE VERSUS DEEP LEARNING

SOURCE: Jimmy Conde, graphic artist.

Transfer Is Both a Means and an End

It can sometimes be confusing to say that the goal of conceptual learning is transfer. When teachers hear this, they often think that this means transfer comes at the end of a unit. We often hear teachers say, *This is great! I teach students about the concepts for a few weeks and then I design an assessment where they have to apply their understanding to a new situation. If they can transfer the idea, we've hit our goal!*

This isn't quite right. If we wait until the end of a unit of study to give students the chance to transfer their understanding to a new situation, we're bound to be disappointed. Students need regular and frequent practice testing out their generalizations and determining how they apply in a new context.

The beauty of teaching through the inquiry cycle, following an iterative process where students investigate the concepts over and over again in new ways, is that it's easy to offer transfer opportunities throughout the unit. Think about it. Students begin with an idea about the relationship between two concepts based on their prior knowledge. Then they test this understanding in a new context during the first inquiry cycle. They're transferring already!

The tricky part is that students are not naturally good at transferring their understanding. Although our brains are wired to draw out conceptual relationships from a set of examples—think of the toddler who learns early on that green vegetables taste bad—we rarely execute this process consciously. Additionally, by the time students reach secondary school they have often stopped expecting school to make sense or have any practical application. Because of this, they need help to become conscious of and deliberately execute the process for conceptual transfer:

1. **Recognize the concepts that apply:** Which concepts are at work in this situation? Which conceptual relationships seem to be shaping this scenario?

2. **Engage prior understanding of the conceptual relationship:** What do I already know to be true about the relationship among these concepts? What specific examples support my understanding?

3. **Determine the extent to which prior understanding applies:** What makes this new situation different from the situations I've studied in the past? Is my generalization likely to hold true in this situation? Which parts of my prior understanding transfer and which don't?

4. **Modify and refine understanding based on the new situation:** How can I reshape my understanding in light of this new situation?

Students often want learning to be black and white. Contradictions and complications are generally unwelcome, and their brains work to sift them out. But a significant understanding of any conceptual relationship requires students to face, and directly deal with, examples and information that don't fit the generalizations they've built. This means that generalizations cannot always be applied wholesale to every new situation and that it is important to pay close attention to what makes a new situation unique.

Here's an example of what we mean. When learning about the concept of revolution, and related concepts of change, stability, injustice, and conflict, students often conclude that *widespread injustice leads people to take major risks for change, resulting in revolution.*

They may look at the Arab Spring, the French Revolution, and the Russian Revolution as separate contexts. In every case, masses of people experienced such deep injustice that they initiated conflict and pressed for revolutionary transformations in their countries. But then they may look at the American Revolution and see a different story altogether. It's impossible to argue that the American colonists experienced objective, widespread mistreatment in the mid-1700s. In fact, scholars argue that they were likely the most free, equal, and prosperous people on the planet at that time. This should grind kids' conceptual gears to a halt. It should cause some intellectual panic! This complicates, and in fact contradicts, their understanding of the concepts.

How do kids reconcile these contradictions? Unfortunately, they tend not to. They simply read the American Revolution the way they want it to be, not the way it was. They imagine oppressive taxation leading people to lose their fortunes. They write bitter paragraphs about how taxes on tea left everyone poor and destroyed the colonists' lives. This, of course, is crazy. There is not a shred of truth in it. But when faced with a complication, they unconsciously iron out the kinks to make the example fit their preexisting theory.

> Transfer can help students unlock new situations by recognizing familiar patterns. At the same time, though, mindless transfer can lead students to misunderstand new phenomena by erasing the unique features at hand.

This is why transfer is so tricky. Transfer can help students unlock new situations by recognizing familiar patterns. At the same time, though, mindless transfer can lead students to misunderstand new phenomena by erasing the unique features at hand.

It is important, then, that teachers design opportunities for students to not just practice transfer but to "fail" at transfer. This means they need to interact with situations where their generalizations will not hold completely true and may even get in the way. Here is one way to do this:

Strategy #10: Transfer and Its Limitations

Consider incorporating this activity into the middle or end of any unit of study. It is important that students have thought about the concepts and have formed some generalizations prior to this activity.

1. Discuss the meaning of transfer with students. This term can get cloudy, so we find it helpful to talk about three aspects of transfer:
   - **Analyzing:** Transferring understanding means you can break a new situation down into its component parts according to predictable patterns (*e.g., calculus students can determine the acceleration of a car by recognizing the relationship among speed, time, and distance on a graph*).
   - **Making predictions:** Transferring understanding means you can predict the likely outcome or impact of a new situation (*e.g., ecology students anticipate that a decline in bee population will cause major consequences for other species living in the same habitat*).
   - **Solving a problem:** Transferring understanding means you can come up with solutions to a problem based on your understanding of the concepts (*e.g., geography students can offer measures to prevent conflicts over resources based on a deep understanding of how resources and conflict are related*).
2. Ask students to generate a list of ways they could transfer their understanding of the concepts currently being studied. Ask them to think of at least one way they could use their understanding to analyze a new situation, make predictions, or create solutions. Discuss their lists, noting the ways in which transfer is useful.

3. Next, offer students a scenario where their understanding of the concepts is sure to fall short. This will vary by discipline and unit, but the following list of options may help you identify a good example:
   - A mathematical problem of a different type (e.g., a quadratic function when students have been studying linear functions)
   - An anomaly or exception (e.g., a case study of a nation that resolved a deep internal conflict peacefully when students have been studying civil wars)
   - An example that shares some obvious characteristics with previous contexts studied but deep down is very different (e.g., idea of YOLO—"you only live once"—when students have been studying the idea of *carpe diem* in poetry)

4. Ask students to analyze, make predictions, or offer solutions based on their conceptual understanding. Then discuss the accuracy of their application. For instance, if students are making predictions, reveal the actual outcome of the situation. Discuss the following questions:
   - What were the limitations of transferring your generalization to this context?
   - What clues in the new context might have signaled to you that your generalization would not apply easily to the situation?
   - What is the danger of mindlessly transferring your understanding without considering the nuances of each individual context or situation?

Conclusion

In this chapter we've offered some strategies to help teachers design lesson segments that align with conceptual learning goals. But we hope our readers understand that these strategies are just a starting point to help them envision the many possible ways that students can experience conceptual learning. More important than the individual strategies are the underlying principles outlined at the start of the chapter. They are worth repeating:

1. We need to expose students' **pre-instructional understanding** of the concepts and conceptual relationship.

2. A deep understanding of **each concept by itself** is necessary for a sophisticated understanding of the relationship among several concepts.

3. Students must **uncover** the conceptual relationship for themselves.

4. **Transfer** is both a means and an end of conceptual learning.

Teachers who understand these principles can easily improvise beyond the strategies provided here to meet the needs of their particular students in a way that suits their preferred teaching style. In Chapter 4 we'll show you how to combine these strategies and sequence lesson components to create dynamic, cohesive learning paths for a variety of unit types.

Chapter Review

- Why is it important to engage students' prior understanding of the concepts at the start of a unit or lesson? What strategies might you employ to do this?

- What can teachers do to develop understanding—not memorization—of new concepts early in a unit of study?

- What is the meaning of the phrase "Uncover → Transfer"? What do these steps look like in the classroom?

- What is the relationship between transfer of learning and deep learning?

CHAPTER 4

....

What Additional Tools Can We Use to Design Lessons?

We've adapted four popular instructional models to further guide the planning process and to ensure students **uncover conceptual relationships.** The most important thing to remember when adapting any instructional tool is to make certain that conceptual understanding is the goal.

Each of these well-liked models has great features aimed to engage students and foster learning that lasts. They are sometimes implemented, however, with the same surface level of understanding as traditional teaching methods. The first step in designing lessons is always identifying the statement of conceptual relationship that represents one of the goals of the unit.

> The most important thing to remember when adapting any instructional tool is to make certain that conceptual understanding is the goal.

The four major steps in any Concept-Based lesson framework follow:

1. Students respond with initial thoughts to **conceptual questions** about the relationship between the concepts.

2. Students explore one or more **specific contexts** that illustrate the nature of the relationship and give them the fact base needed for deep thinking.

3. Students **explain (write, draw, tell, etc.) a statement of conceptual relationship** with evidence from the context to help support and explain the relationship.

4. Students **transfer** their understanding to a new situation.

All of the lesson frameworks in this chapter follow these basic steps, with a few additions added in between the steps. Each framework contains a list of steps with corresponding questions to spur thought, along with a few examples of what it might look like in action. It is extremely important to note that the steps most often occur over multiple class periods, especially when classes are about an hour or less.

Lesson Framework #1: Generating and Testing Hypotheses

Once students have been introduced to the concepts that anchor your unit of study, they are ready to generate and test hypotheses about the relationship among those concepts. In his book, *The Art and Science of Teaching,* Robert Marzano (2007) noted that providing opportunities for students to generate hypotheses and test them—through experimental inquiry, problem solving, decision making, or investigation tasks—has been proven to produce substantial learning gains. This is likely because the process of generating and testing hypotheses engages students' preconceptions about the concepts (their initial hypotheses will reveal their preconceptions about how the concepts relate to each other) and asks them to become aware of the ways in which new knowledge challenges or confirms their prior understanding.

Generating and testing hypotheses about conceptual relationships generally happen through these steps:

1. Students write an initial response to conceptual questions (their preconceptions).

2. Students learn a little about a specific context, enough to generate a hypothesis (topic/context/facts).

3. Students develop a hypothesis about the conceptual relationship in light of the topic.

4. Students learn more about the topic in order to test their hypotheses.

5. Students abstract to an improved statement of conceptual relationship supported by evidence from the context (Steps 4 and 5 can be repeated several times).

6. Students transfer this understanding to a new situation.

7. Students reflect on growth in thinking and understanding.

Figure 4.1 provides corresponding question prompts to stimulate thoughtful planning and examples of what it might look like in the classroom.

FIGURE 4.1   GENERATING AND TESTING HYPOTHESES LESSON FRAMEWORK

Lesson Principle	Questions to Ask Yourself	Might Look Like
1. Start with **conceptual questions** that target the statement of conceptual relationships of the unit.	• What conceptual relationships are at the heart of this unit? • How can I create conceptual questions that engage students and allow for deep thought right away? • What questions will allow me to gauge students' pre-instructional understanding of the concepts?	• Students record their initial thoughts about conceptual relationships in their journal. • Groups draw nonlinguistic representations of the concept on chart paper and gallery walk to see the breadth of the class's thinking. • Small groups discuss conceptual questions and teacher observes. • Teacher provides a variety of sample relationship statements and students explain which one aligns with their thinking and why.
2. Provide enough **background** on the topic of inquiry in order to make a hypothesis (e.g., background on the author or text, a preview of a historical example).	• In what context will students investigate the concepts? • What background information would allow students to generate useful hypotheses about the concept in this context? • How could I preview the topic in a way that intrigues students and sets the stage for inquiry? How can I set up a "mystery" for students to solve?	• Students explore stations or conduct a gallery walk of intriguing images that introduce basics of the topic. • Students give a short lecture or presentation explaining the basic background. • Students perform a dramatic read-aloud of a key passage of text or quote about the historical event/figure. • Students read a "fact sheet" with four to five key details. • Students brainstorm background knowledge in a KWL chart.

(Continued)

FIGURE 4.1   GENERATING AND TESTING HYPOTHESES LESSON FRAMEWORK (CONTINUED)

Lesson Principle	Questions to Ask Yourself	Might Look Like
3. Students **generate hypotheses** about the topic/text based on current understanding of conceptual relationships.	• How can students use their current understanding of the concepts to generate hypotheses about the topic/text?	• Students brainstorm hypotheses about the topic/text on sticky notes and categorize them as a group. • Students list as many hypotheses as possible in their journal and then circle the best one. • Pairs discuss and come to consensus on a hypothesis they will test together.
4. Provide texts/experiences that allow students to **test their hypotheses** about the topic through a specific context.	• What experiences would allow students to test their hypotheses and gain a more nuanced or sophisticated understanding of the relationship between concepts? • Which inquiry strategies will best help students test their hypotheses about this topic?	• Students engage in individual reading, marking text for evidence for or against the hypothesis, followed by a group discussion of the text and evidence found. • The whole class watches a video or lecture and records evidence for/against the hypothesis; pairs discuss the viability of the hypothesis and revise it if necessary. • Students research information online and collect evidence for/against the hypothesis. • Students rotate through stations and gather evidence to test the hypothesis.
5. Ask students to **generalize about the concepts** in light of what they learned about the topic.	• How could students use their learning about the topic to create a transferable understanding about the concepts in general?	• **Students write statements to express relationships between concepts.** Additionally … • Students draw nonlinguistic representations of the conceptual relationship and explain their thinking to a partner. • Synectics—students consider a variety of images and choose which one best represents the conceptual relationship.

Lesson Principle	Questions to Ask Yourself	Might Look Like
6. Have students **refine and test their statements of conceptual relationship** (and peers' statements).	• How can students increase the clarity, accuracy, precision, depth, breadth, relevance, significance, and fairness of their statements? • How can students use facts to support their statements?	• Students ask "why?" "how?" and "so what?" to improve precision and significance of statements. • Students list facts and examples **outside the context studied** that support their generalizations. • Students read others' statements and refine or support them with evidence. • Students create structure of knowledge diagrams to show how they built their statement. • Students perform research to further test and refine their statements.
7. Ask students to **reflect** on learning and explain transferability of their statements of conceptual relationships.	• How can students gain awareness of their learning and the usefulness of their new understanding of the concepts? • How can I help students track their own growth in thinking and understanding?	• Students return to their original thoughts about the concept and compare them to their new thoughts. • Students complete an exit slip describing how their understanding has changed. • Students track their growth on a novice to expert scale/rubric (see Chapter 5) and explain what happened in their brains to make this progress. • Students name the points of the lesson when they were doing "complex" or "deep" thinking and explain what this felt like. • Pairs brainstorm situations where they could use their new idea (transferability). • Students explain how a partner helped them push their thinking or led them to a "breakthrough."

We've included a few examples from secondary classrooms to help teachers visualize this framework in the context of real classrooms. There are social studies, music, and science examples.

Example from a geography lesson:

> Concepts: Nations, resources, scarcity
>
> Conceptual relationships: Scarcity or mismatch between supply and demand in resources causes conflicts between interdependent nations.
>
> When interdependent nations cooperate to share scarce resources for the greater good, conflict can be reduced and economic opportunities strengthened.
>
> Context: Sudan and Egypt's relationship over scarce freshwater from the Nile River

1. Start with a conceptual question: What happens among nations when shared resources become scarce?

2. Provide context and share background information: There is a water crisis along the Nile River. We will look at two nations in particular, Egypt and South Sudan, to see what is happening between them. Egypt is more powerful than South Sudan. Water flows from South Sudan to Egypt.

3. Generate a hypothesis: What do you think is going to happen in this situation?

4. Test the hypothesis: Students evaluate and learn what is really happening based on the potential solutions.

5. Generalize: Students edit and enhance their statements based on the context of the Nile. They must use evidence from the situation to defend their statement.

6. Transfer: Explain that there is a similar situation between China and Japan with the Senkaku Islands, which have natural gas, oil, and fresh fish. Ask this: Does your statement hold true here? Enhance your statement to account for the nuanced differences between the two situations.

7. Reflect: Students practice metacognition on how their thinking improved in clarity, significance, depth, and relevance over the course of the lesson.

Example from a music class (by Roberto Pfizenmaier):

> Concepts: Music elements of tone, rhythm, harmony, sound
>
> Conceptual relationships: The elements of music work together to create something pleasing to the ears of the listener. Emphasis of certain musical elements over others characterizes time periods or genres of music.
>
> Context: Renaissance period

1. How do the elements of music create beauty? What is the relationship between the music elements and time periods or genres of music?

2. Learn about music developments during the Renaissance period.

3. Present a musical piece from the time period. Knowing the piece is from the Renaissance and looking only at the lyrics, predict how the elements will be organized. How will the piece sound? What will the musical text look like?

4. Hear the piece from the Renaissance, and check and correct hypotheses.

5. Improve responses to the initial conceptual question in light of the piece.

6. Transfer to a new piece during the Baroque period.

7. Reflect on how your understanding of musical elements improved by listening to the Renaissance and Baroque period pieces.

Example from a chemistry class (by Georgina Carey and Max Fox):

Concepts: Structure, matter, persistence

Statement of conceptual relationship: The molecular structure of matter dictates its persistence in the environment.

1. Students write an initial response to conceptual questions (their preconceptions): Why do some substances persist longer than others in the environment?

2. Students learn about a specific context (topic): They are given samples of substances with ionic, covalent, and metallic bonds. Students learn about the nature of covalent and ionic bonding and their properties by looking at these samples. They develop a hypothesis about the concepts in light of the topic.

3. Students generate a hypothesis: Will covalent or ionic bonds dissolve in water?

4. Students learn more about the context: Through an experiment they discover ionic bonds will dissolve in water.

5. Students abstract to an improved statement of conceptual relationship supported by evidence from the experiment.

6. Students transfer their understanding to another task: Students transfer their knowledge about molecular structure to plastic. They make plastic in class and see its large molecular structure and explain why it persists so long in the environment.

7. Students reflect on growth in thinking and understanding: They look back at their original responses to the question and reflect on how their increased understanding of science through the experiment and the creation of plastic in class has helped them to improve their answer.

Lesson Framework #2: Workshop Model for Complex Processes

The workshop model has been common practice for English language arts classrooms for many years. It has more recently made its way into math classrooms. The idea is to provide as much classroom time as possible to students practicing skills for complex processes while the teacher provides feedback. It is not too different from the idea behind "flipped classrooms"—where students watch videos of their teacher demonstrating a skill at home and then come to school and practice it where the teacher can provide feedback. The flip is between where students receive explanation (at home) and where they practice (at school). With the workshop model, the teacher provides a minilesson at the start of class and then the rest of the class time is for practicing the strategy presented in the minilesson.

One of the greatest proponents of the workshop model is literacy expert Chris Tovani (2011), who said the following:

> Just like athletes on the field who do the majority of the work during practice, students in my classroom do the majority of the work by reading, writing and thinking during class. By organizing my time using the workshop model every day, all year long, I can ensure that their reading, writing and thinking are getting better. (p. 39)

This is a particularly effective way to design lessons for subjects that are process oriented, such as the arts and languages. While mathematics has important processes, strategies, and skills, it is essential that lessons on the knowledge side complement the process side. This cannot be the only lesson design structure used in mathematics classes. Other disciplines such as science and social studies can use this model for their statements of conceptual relationship that are from the Structure of Process— the complex processes that disciplinarians *do* to carry out the discipline. See Figure 4.2 for an example in science.

FIGURE 4.2   SCIENCE COMPLEX PROCESS EXAMPLE

Science example:
Scientists and engineers plan and carry out investigations individually and collaboratively, identifying independent and dependent variables and controls.

The idea is to provide a minilesson on one specific strategy or skill that is essential to carrying out a complex process. For example, if the complex process is *argumentative writing*, you might focus first on *making a strong claim* and do a minilesson on just that part of argumentative writing. Next you would allow students to practice that skill first before introducing, say, how to write *strong reasoning, provide supporting evidence,* and *make counterclaims to those opposed to your ideas.* Each of those aspects of argumentative writing would be broken down into distinct lessons or a few lessons before moving on.

The purpose of calling it a minilesson means that it is both specific and brief. Students then use the remaining class time, which should be the majority of the lesson, to practice this skill or strategy. The majority of class time is dedicated to student practice and allows time for the teacher to provide specific, positive feedback. Figure 4.3 provides a framework to create a workshop model lesson plan that builds conceptual understanding.

FIGURE 4.3 WORKSHOP MODEL LESSON FRAMEWORK

Lesson Principle	Questions to Ask Yourself	Might Look Like
1. Opening: Conceptual questions	• What conceptual relationships are at the heart of this unit? • How can I create conceptual questions that engage students and allow for deep thought right away? • What questions will allow me to gauge students' pre-instructional understanding of the concepts? • How can students connect the current goal to previous learning? • How can students use their current understanding of the concepts to connect to the day's goal? • How can students articulate the connection between the day's strategy to the overall complex process?	• Students record their initial thoughts about conceptual relationships in their journal. • Groups draw nonlinguistic representations of the concept on chart paper and gallery walk to see the breadth of the class's thinking. • Small groups discuss conceptual questions and teacher observes. • Teacher provides variety of sample relationship statements and students explain which one aligns with their thinking and why. • Pairs discuss and come to consensus on how today's goal links to their previous learning.
2. Minilesson	• How can I model the specific strategy or skill in a way that will clearly illustrate the *thinking moves* for this strategy or skill? • How will students engage right away with the demonstration? • How will students link the demonstration to the day's work? • How will students link the minilesson to the overall complex process?	• Teacher conducts a "think-aloud" to demonstrate what he or she is thinking about while executing the strategy or skill. • Students interview teacher to find out more about how he or she completes this strategy. • Students pair-share what they noticed during the demonstration. • Students watch a video that introduces a new strategy or skills for a complex process. • Students write an explanation of how to do it in their own words; teacher circulates and corrects any errors.

(Continued)

FIGURE 4.3 WORKSHOP MODEL LESSON FRAMEWORK (CONTINUED)

Lesson Principle	Questions to Ask Yourself	Might Look Like
3. **Work time**	• How will students practice the strategy or skill? • What specific context(s) will we use to allow for practice? • How will I provide guidance and feedback as they practice? • How will we celebrate success and progress made?	• Students evaluate an example of this strategy or skill. • Students practice and then evaluate their own work. • Peers give each other feedback on their practice work. • Students choose how they will practice the skill or strategy.
4. **Generalize and debrief**	• How can students connect the current goal to previous learning? • How can students use their learning about the specific skill or strategy to write transferable statements of conceptual relationship about the complex process?	• Students explain how today's goal relates to the complex process. • Students write statements about the relationship between today's concept and yesterday's concept.
5. **Transfer**	• How can students evaluate the transferability of their statements of conceptual relationship?	• Pairs brainstorm situations when they could use their new idea (transferability). • Teacher presents a new situation for students to transfer their understanding of the skill. • Pairs evaluate an example of a statement and whether it is transferable to a new situation.

TOOLS FOR TEACHING CONCEPTUAL UNDERSTANDING, SECONDARY

Lesson Framework #3: Project-Based Learning

Learning centered around projects often provides meaning for students and is one way to make learning more organized, authentic, and less fragmented from day to day. Many schools are adopting this method of instruction as a means to motivate students and make learning more relevant and inclusive. It is completely compatible with Concept-Based Curriculum and Instruction. We just need to be very careful to articulate conceptual goals from the start and keep them as the focus throughout.

We turn to the Buck Institute for Education's Gold Standards for Project-Based Learning to craft this lesson framework and provide guidance on how to blend these two important educational endeavors. The Buck Institute for Education provides a clear definition of project-based learning: "Project Based Learning is a teaching method in which students gain knowledge and skills by working for an extended period of time to investigate and respond to an engaging and complex question, problem, or challenge" ("What Is Project-Based," n.d.).

The Buck Institute also provides clear design elements, which are aligned to Concept-Based Curriculum and Instruction in the following ways:

1. Projects begin with clear knowledge, understanding, and skills, aligning to Erickson's KUDs (the skills are what students "do," which becomes the D in KUD; Erickson et al., 2017).

2. Projects use an inquiry or inductive process to guide students toward discovery of understanding.

3. Projects start with and maintain a question or challenge rather than a statement to engage students and turn on the brain.

Consider each element of Gold Standard Project-Based Learning listed in Figure 4.4 (see page 78), as well as the slight modifications we make in applying this approach to Concept-Based units.

It is important to realize that project-based learning does not happen in a single, stand-alone lesson. Therefore, a framework for planning Concept-Based projects should be used to design an entire unit of study, not just a lesson or two. There is just no way to build knowledge through sustained inquiry or to critique and revise processes and products in a few days. We suggest using this model for a three- to four-week project, minimum, and often much longer.

When planning a Concept-Based project, we find it useful to create a student-facing document that outlines the project, establishes some criteria for success, and identifies major deadlines. Create a one-page letter to students that frames the challenge of the project. We love to use a modified version of the GRASPS model created by Wiggins and McTighe (2005) as a guideline, adding "concepts" to keep us focused on our conceptual goals:

(Text continues on page 79.)

FIGURE 4.4 COMBINING PROJECT-BASED LEARNING (PBL) AND CONCEPT-BASED CURRICULUM AND INSTRUCTION

Gold Standard PBL Element	Traditional PBL	Concept-Based PBL Modifications
Key Knowledge, Understanding, and Success Skills	The project is focused on student learning goals, including standards-based content and skills such as critical thinking/problem solving, collaboration, and self-management.	The project is focused on **conceptual** learning goals, in addition to standards-based content and skills such as critical thinking/problem solving, collaboration, and self-management.
Challenging Problem or Question	The project is framed by a meaningful problem to solve or a question to answer, at the appropriate level of challenge.	The project is framed by a **conceptual** question or meaningful problem to be solved using conceptual understanding.
Sustained Inquiry	Students engage in a rigorous, extended process of asking questions, finding resources, and applying information.	Students inquire into several different **contexts to inform conceptual understanding** and apply to solving the challenge, problem, or question.
Authenticity	The project features real-world context, tasks and tools, quality standards, or impact—or speaks to students' personal concerns, interests, and issues in their lives.	Authenticity involves **transfer of conceptual understanding** to a real-world context.
Student Voice & Choice	Students make some decisions about the project, including how they work and what they create.	Students can make choices about the different contexts they investigate and may arrive at their own unique conceptual understandings in addition to other choices in the project.
Reflection	Students and teachers reflect on learning, the effectiveness of their inquiry and project activities, the quality of student work, obstacles and how to overcome them.	Students also reflect on the **evolution of their conceptual understanding** and effectiveness of transferring this understanding to a new situation.
Critique & Revision	Students give, receive, and use feedback to improve their process and products.	Student critique and revision include a critique and revision of conceptual understanding and effectiveness of transfer.
Public Product	Students make their project work public by explaining, displaying, and/or presenting it to people beyond the classroom.	Concepts and conceptual relationships are made explicit in the public product.

SOURCE: (first two columns) "What Is Project Based Learning (PBL)?" (n.d.).

TOOLS FOR TEACHING CONCEPTUAL UNDERSTANDING, SECONDARY

- **Concepts:** Name the concepts that students will be investigating in this project.

- **Goal:** State a clear goal so students know what they need to do with their understanding of the concepts.

- **Role:** Assign students a real-world role or perspective.

- **Audience:** Describe the real-world audience students should keep in mind when designing their final product.

- **Situation:** Situate the question or problem in a specific context and describe it briefly.

- **Public product or performance:** Tell students what they are expected to create (an essay, skit, website, documentary, business proposal, etc.).

- **Standards for success:** Communicate the criteria for successful completion of the project. Consider including a rubric to measure the quality of the final product as well as checklists that outline the essential components you expect to be included.

Here's an example from a geography classroom. Note that while the acronym C-GRASPS helps educators remember the essential elements for framing a project, this is not necessarily the most natural order for explaining the elements to students. See if you can identify each element in the following project:

> *Water is a vital resource to human life. Experts recommend that each person drink two liters of water every day to maintain good health. Additionally, we need water to nourish the crops we grow for food. As the population of the earth increases, water becomes scarcer, and it becomes tougher for all people to have access to the water they need to survive. Recently, Ethiopia decided to build a dam on the Nile River, which supplies fresh water to Ethiopia, Sudan, and Egypt. Sudan and Egypt have complained that the new dam will restrict their access to the water they need. Imagine you are a special advisor to the United Nations investigating the relationship among scarcity, power, and conflict. Research at least three other situations in which control of a scarce resource caused a disagreement among nations. What generalizations can you draw from these situations? Based on past examples, what is likely to happen once the Ethiopian dam is constructed? Create a short presentation to the United Nations based on your findings. Be sure that you provide specific evidence to support your generalizations and conclusions. Also, be prepared to answer questions from U.N. officials after your presentation. We will role-play the presentations but your proposals will be shared with the real United Nations.*

Teachers may choose to include the grading rubric alongside the document framing the C-GRASPS of the task. Alternately, it is sometimes beneficial to include students in the process of determining criteria for success. In the previous example, for instance, the teacher may have students watch a video of a speaker addressing the United Nations and ask what a good presentation should look like.

Once you have a vision for the project, consider the following instructional principles and steps in Figure 4.5 as you plan for instruction:

FIGURE 4.5   PROJECT-BASED LESSON FRAMEWORK

Lesson Principle	Questions to Ask Yourself	Might Look Like
1. "Hook" students by introducing them to the conceptual question to be answered or problem to be solved (sometimes called a "launch").	• What conceptual relationships do I want students to uncover in this project? • How can I make this question or problem relevant, urgent, and interesting? • How can I get kids to "wonder" about the question or problem without feeding it to them? • How can I connect the concepts to students' emotions, personal interests and concerns, culture, or identity to draw them in?	• Students explore ideas via a gallery walk of photos, statistics, and quotes related to the problem to be solved (e.g., migrant crisis in Europe, global water shortages). • Watch a short video or read a short story through which the question might surface (e.g., read E. E. Cummings's poem and ponder the role of punctuation, grammar, and word order in writing). • Discuss a real-life or school-based scenario that correlates to the concepts (e.g., discussing a mother appeasing a toddler throwing a tantrum in a candy store before inquiring into the foreign policy of appeasing Hitler in the 1930s). • Partner with a local organization to extend a challenge or pose a question to students (e.g., a representative from a local watershed protection society comes to class to enlist student help in reducing pollution in local waterways). • Distribute a written overview of the project to students, complete with rubric and deadlines, to help them envision the challenge.
2. Help students plan their inquiry and build background knowledge.	• How much support and direction will I provide to students during the inquiry process?	• Students brainstorm possible approaches to the question or problem as a whole class while the teacher scribes on the board.

Lesson Principle	Questions to Ask Yourself	Might Look Like
2. (Continued from above)	• Which contexts should all students study? Which other contexts might students choose to investigate as part of their inquiry? • What resources would best help students deeply inquire into the question or problem?	• Provide a sample research calendar to each group and ask them to modify it or divide tasks among them. • Supply a list of resources for each context (books, videos, articles, images, etc.) to get students started. • Help students brainstorm ways to extend their inquiry: interviewing experts, taking a field trip, designing an experiment, conducting an opinion poll, etc. • Give students a written research guide that outlines your expectations (specific contexts they must study, optional contexts, types of acceptable sources).
3. Monitor the student inquiry process and guide student reflection.	• What scaffolding will students need to help them conduct their own research? • How will I serve as a coach for each group during the inquiry process? • What questions will I pose to students to challenge them? • How will I make sure students are focused on the concepts? • When and how will students reflect on their understanding and the inquiry process?	• Provide graphic organizers to help students organize information. • Ask students to keep a journal of their research (they should summarize their findings and also reflect on the inquiry process); provide comments and feedback. • "Interview" each group about the concepts at various intervals throughout the inquiry process.
4. Support students as they construct high-quality products through critique and revision.	• How will students know what quality work looks like? • How can I ensure that students thoughtfully critique their own and each other's work? • How will students know how to revise or strengthen weak areas of their product?	• Provide rubrics, checklists, and models of exemplary work. • Ask students to use formal critique and feedback protocols when responding to each other's work. • Bring in experts to provide feedback based on the standards of quality in your field.

(Continued)

FIGURE 4.5 PROJECT-BASED LESSON FRAMEWORK (CONTINUED)

Lesson Principle	Questions to Ask Yourself	Might Look Like
5. Organize students to publish or present their products to a real-world audience.	• Who is the primary audience for this work? How can I help students get the attention of their target audience? • Can we present these products off campus or outside of school hours? • How will students prepare to discuss their work with others?	• Invite the school community—parents, teachers, other students—to a "gallery opening" or "invention fair" with student products on display. • Conduct a "teach-in" where students present their conclusions to others in order to inform or persuade. • Organize a panel of experts—lawyers, engineers, environmentalists, college professors—to respond to and evaluate student speeches. • Post student videos to a YouTube channel or create a website to convey student findings to the outside world.
6. Provide opportunities for reflection about the content and the process.	• How will students reflect on the conceptual relationships they uncovered, the facts that support these relationships, and the significance of their new understanding? • How will students reflect on their learning process? • How will students reflect on their role within the group and the group dynamic? • How will students reflect on the quality of their final product?	• Ask students to write journal entries using the prompt: "At the start of the project I thought…but then…so now I think…" • Have students record video blogs where they verbally express their reflections (similar to a reality show "confessional"). • Require students to write letters to their group-mates, the audience of their product, or you (the teacher) to explain how these people contributed to their learning. • Have groups write a group reflection in the form advice for next year's students. • Have students list "lessons learned" on sticky notes and then categorize and debrief them as a class.

Project-based learning is a powerful way for students to uncover conceptual relationships because it puts their conceptual understanding to real-world use. To maximize the impact of your project, be sure to avoid these common pitfalls:

- It's easy to plan a project that is real-world, interesting, or hands-on without requiring deep investigation or transfer of the concepts. If you are new to this, it might help to start with the concepts and contexts you would normally teach in a unit, rather than starting with the real-world scenario that requires transfer of conceptual understanding. Just be sure to include conceptual understanding and evidence as categories in your rubric or scoring scheme.

- Too much student independence can lead to misunderstandings, as students tend to rush through the investigatory phase of the project to focus more on the product. Set up checkpoints or benchmarks and help guide the pace of each group's work and to formally assess student understanding as they move along.

- Too little student independence defeats the purpose of the project-based model. Students need time and space to make mistakes and then to learn from them as they refine their understanding and product through feedback. When you notice students making mistakes, resist the urge to tell students what to do or think. Instead, ask questions and provide feedback that allows students to figure out how to improve on their own.

- Remember that the project-based model is a way of designing an entire unit of study, meaning that students must learn the required content and develop conceptual understanding *through* the project. Assigning a project at the end of a unit, after the required learning has already taken place, is not project-based learning but rather an assessment of learning otherwise achieved. Both are valid classroom tools, but the structure here is meant to support project-based learning, not project-based assessment.

Lesson Framework #4: Personalized Learning

We are encouraged by the trend of learning adapted to the pace, needs, goals, interests, and motivations of students rather than students constantly adapting to the average-oriented, one-size-fits all instruction. We've included this lesson framework because personalized learning is a valuable method of teaching and learning. It is a relatively new and trendy phenomenon; therefore, we will take a moment to frame what it means to us.

First, what is personalized learning? Many people think of it as "learning at your own pace." We think this is an overly simplistic view. We prefer to think of it as each student *making meaning* for himself or herself which is aligned to the philosophy of inductive or constructivist teaching. In this mode of thinking, it becomes clear that simply checking off tasks on a playlist that feels more like a "to-do" list without a demonstration of deep understanding is not exactly revolutionary or great learning—even if you can check off those boxes in a different order or at a different rate than the student next to you.

Personalized learning is often presented as synonymous with technology. We value the role of technology in helping our young people learn better and faster, but personalized learning does not have to be dependent on technology. We've added alternatives to learning exclusively from a laptop or tablet in this lesson framework.

Another, related tension with personalized learning lies in the importance of learning in a social context. Humans are social animals and there is a lot of research to support students discussing ideas and learning from each other, which is hard to do if your path involves a lot of individual time with a screen. Also worth noting is that, at the time of this writing, very little technology can provide valuable feedback on the *quality* of student work. Tech can tell us "yes, you got it right" or "no, you didn't," but we know that deeper learning requires more than that. Therefore, we caution zealous implementers of personalized learning to be sure to include lots of human expert feedback on student work as well as time for kids to work together to construct meaning.

What troubles us the most, however, is that missing from the hype of truly transforming teaching and learning is that the *goals* often remain surface level. This is why we assert that a curriculum must go beyond the topic level before we even begin to talk about personalizing instruction. There is sometimes a corresponding component of eschewing standardization and adding new goals such as critical thinking and creativity. It is crucial to remember that *innovation requires expertise and a fundamental understanding of at least one discipline.* Let's not throw the baby out with the bathwater! That's the value of Concept-Based Curriculum.

Personalization often offers students more voice and choice in their learning. Concept-Based Curriculum naturally allows for more personalization, particularly in the contexts that students explore in order to arrive at the conceptual relationships. Compare the following two attempts at deeper learning for an English language arts class (see Figure 4.6). Why does the Concept-Based unit naturally allow for more student choice?

Through conceptual questions, students are able to choose texts to read to arrive at their own conclusions. Each student could be reading an entirely different book,

FIGURE 4.6   TOPIC VERSUS CONCEPT-BASED UNIT

Topic-Based Unit	Concept-Based Unit
Students will analyze the character development and universal themes of *Romeo and Juliet*.	Students will uncover and transfer the understanding that *authors develop complexity of characters through dialogue, plot, and descriptive text.* Conceptual Question: How do authors develop complexity of characters?

but with a focused goal of conceptual relationship, the teacher could facilitate rich discussions using the conceptual questions.

A diverse group funded by the Bill & Melinda Gates Foundation gathered to define personalized learning. "A Working Definition of Personalized Learning" (2014) outlined four key areas:

1. Learner profiles: Each student has an up-to-date record of his or her individual strengths, needs, motivations, and goals.

2. Personal learning paths: All students are held to clear, high expectations, but each student follows a customized path that responds and adapts based on his or her individual learning progress, motivations, and goals.

3. Competency-based progression: Each student's progress toward clearly defined goals is continually assessed. A student advances and earns credit as soon as he or she demonstrates mastery.

4. Flexible learning environments: Student needs drive the design of the learning environment. All operational elements—staffing plans, space utilization, and time allocation—respond and adapt to support students in achieving their goals.

A really important characteristic of personalized learning is *learning pathways*. The idea is to disassemble the learning hierarchy of certain lessons before others, place them all in front of students at the same time, and allow the students to learn not only at their own pace but in their own order. In the context of conceptual teaching and learning, we can plan different ways students collect information that will help them answer the conceptual questions. See Figure 4.7 for the framework for personalized learning.

These four lesson frameworks demonstrate ways in which we can ensure different instructional models can be aligned to Concept-Based Curriculum design. As long as conceptual understanding is the goal and students use a fact base from a specific context to uncover the conceptual relationship, you are on the right track as a conceptual teacher. The more practice students have at transferring their understanding to new situations, the deeper their learning.

Sample Instructional Calendar

Most schools use two common written curriculum documents: unit planners outlining the goals of the unit and usually the summative assessment and daily lesson planners. At the risk of adding to the long list of things teachers must produce, we advocate the use of a simple calendar that at least roughly sketches out the sequence of lessons and learning experiences. It's not etched in stone, as we must respond to the learning needs of the students. But it provides guidance to ensure we will have enough time for all of the learning goals.

FIGURE 4.7 PERSONALIZED LEARNING LESSON FRAMEWORK

Lesson Principle	Questions to Ask Yourself	Might Look Like
1. Start with **conceptual questions** that target the statement of conceptual relationships of the unit.	<ul><li>What conceptual relationships are at the heart of this unit?</li><li>How can I create conceptual questions that engage students and allow for deep thought right away?</li><li>What questions will allow me to gauge students' pre-instructional understanding of the concepts?</li></ul>	<ul><li>Students record their initial thoughts about conceptual relationships in their journal.</li><li>Groups draw nonlinguistic representations of the concept on chart paper and gallery walk to see the breadth of the class's thinking.</li><li>Small groups discuss conceptual questions and teacher observes.</li><li>Teacher provides a variety of sample relationship statements and students explain which one aligns with their thinking and why.</li></ul>
2. Collect data for the **learner profile**.	<ul><li>What choices might I offer students that cater to their interests, strengths, motivations, and needs?</li><li>How can I use their personal goals in planning the instructional portion of this unit?</li><li>How can I involve students in the planning of the instructional portion of this unit?</li></ul>	<ul><li>Students rank a list of possible contexts that target the conceptual relationships.</li><li>Provide a list of skills associated with the unit and have students sort them based on which are current strengths and which need improvement.</li><li>Students rank their interest in different potential activities for the learner pathways.</li></ul>

Lesson Principle	Questions to Ask Yourself	Might Look Like
3. Brainstorm different potential **learner paths.**	• What choices might I offer students that cater to their interests, strengths, motivations, and needs? • What resources already exist that help build background knowledge and understanding for this unit? • What do I need to create in order to build background knowledge or understanding? • How can I be creative in providing unique and varied experiences that will help students uncover the conceptual relationships? • How can I train people or edit resources in order to build conceptual understanding?	• Create a playlist for the unit and have students move at their own pace to uncover the conceptual relationship. • Students choose between one-on-one tutoring, online learning, or small group instruction that will help them uncover the conceptual relationship. • Students interview different experts about the conceptual relationship of the unit. • Students complete internships as the specific context to better understand the conceptual relationships of the unit. • Students conduct their own research to uncover the conceptual relationships of the unit.
4. Determine how students will demonstrate **mastery** and **progress.**	• How can students frequently measure their progress? • How can students use the data on the formative assessments to set goals and move at their own pace? • What different modalities (essay, video, etc.) can students use to demonstrate progress and mastery? • What is acceptable for mastery of this unit and what will early completers do once they demonstrate mastery?	• Create formative assessments in advance and allow students to complete them frequently. • Create a rubric that allows for multiple modes of performance (video, essay, 3-D design) • Students use formative assessments to determine their pace. • Students choose among several novel situations to explain their understanding. • Early completers design their own project for deepening their understanding or increasing capacity from their needs list.

(Continued)

FIGURE 4.7 PERSONALIZED LEARNING LESSON FRAMEWORK (CONTINUED)

Lesson Principle	Questions to Ask Yourself	Might Look Like
5. Determine how students will **transfer** understanding to a new, complex situation.	• How will students test their statements of conceptual relationships in new contexts?	• Students pair up to test their statements in each other's contexts. • Students choose different contexts to test their relationship. • Peers evaluate each other's relationships. • Mentors provide new contexts to test the relationships. • Pairs brainstorm situations where they could use their new idea (transferability).
6. Think creatively about the **learning environment** and allocation of **resources.**	• What staffing roles will maximize student choice and variance in pacing for this unit? • How can I efficiently use time to allow students to pursue their own interests and goals for this unit? • How can we build connection with other students and adults in this unit? • What community resources are available?	• Tutors provide one-on-one or small group instruction. • Students report to off-site locations instead of coming to school. • A variety of experts come to school, and students rotate through different stations to collect evidence for the conceptual questions. • Students visit the local library to collect evidence for the conceptual questions. • Parents donate supplies to allow hands-on discovery of the conceptual relationships.
7. Determine ways to **evaluate** and **adapt** to learner needs.	• How often will I solicit student feedback on the status of the unit? • How can I adapt learner pathways, resources, and the environment to meet the needs of the students?	• Teachers meet weekly to discuss each student's progress and brainstorm ways to adapt learner pathways. • Students meet weekly with teacher one-on-one to discuss their progress and brainstorm ways to adapt learner pathways.

And at the risk of the reader thinking we advocate one discrete way of doing this—*which we don't*—we've included a sample unit calendar to illustrate how one might approach sequencing lessons in a Concept-Based classroom. See Figure 4.8. for a sample unit calendar for a Grade 9 class on social protest movements. It only utilizes the Generating and Testing Hypotheses Lesson Framework from this chapter, but it also uses several strategies from other chapters. The summative assessment asks students to research and create a historical account of a past protest movement, demonstrating their understanding of the relationship among change, power, ideology, and modes of protest.

This sample unit calendar is meant to help the reader visualize how you might plan a sequence of lessons for a Concept-Based unit—but it is only one example of a million ways to organize instruction. Notice that there is a balance of memorization practice and deeper inquiry into the nature of the relationship as well as specific time to teach the skills required for the summative assessment.

Balancing Conceptual Thinking, Skills Practice, Memorization, and Review

Many teachers worry about the amount of time that instruction for conceptual understanding takes, especially compared with traditional instruction. We used to think that the depth of study into a concept and corresponding topics inevitably meant that we had to spend more time with fewer topics, which was scary. But the better we got at teaching this way, we realized students learn *more* factual content because they actually remember what they've learned and are able to make insightful connections throughout the year demonstrating a depth of understanding.

In fact, we were forced to confront the **myth** that so many of us hold dear: *If we cover material (e.g., tell students something or go over it in class), they will learn it.* This is something many teachers are convinced is true despite so much evidence to the contrary. It may feel more efficient in the short term to spoon-feed students with information or explain step-by-step how to do something. But when they lack depth of understanding they either repeat incorrectly, partially, or forget. Anyone teaching for longer than two months has seen this. Two lessons later, one week later, one month later, the following school year—we are repeatedly shocked by what students either misunderstand, partially understand, or forget.

> When students lack depth of understanding they either repeat incorrectly, partially, or forget.

Consider the metaphors explained in this short excerpt from *The Art of Redesigning Instruction* (Paul, n.d.):

> When we teach in "mother robin" fashion—trying to mentally chew up everything for our students so we can put it into their intellectual beaks to swallow—students tend to become, if I can slightly mix my metaphor,

FIGURE 4.8 SAMPLE UNIT CALENDAR

Introduction to **conceptual learning** and **intellectual growth** *How can I improve the quality of my thinking? What are my intellectual goals for this unit?* -Growth mindset activity -Personalize and begin using intellectual journals -Student goal setting in journal -Introduction to conceptual language using an example from last year's content -Teacher think aloud about the relationship between two previously studied concepts	Introduction to **concepts** of change and power ***What is the relationship between*** *change and power?* -Pre-assessment on concepts and their relationship -Examples and non-examples of change and power to create definitions (concept attainment) -Explore a specific context that illustrates the relationship between the concepts -Return to question to correct and deepen understanding	**Models** and **rubric** for summative task *What is the ultimate goal for this unit? What does success look like? How can I get there?* -Contrast surface and deep learning -Evaluate exemplar and non-exemplar work on a related but different question using the rubric -Student goal setting in journal -Teacher provides feedback based on pre-assessment and explicitly corrects misunderstandings
Memory building *How can I best retain new information for this unit? What surface level learning will allow me to deepen my understanding and transfer my learning?* **What is the impact** of *different modes of power on dominant ideologies?* -Mini-lesson on strategies for memorization/automaticity -Academic vocabulary games for culture, subculture, dominant ideology, revolution, and innovation -Students record level of recall -Students select strategy to build habit	**Deepen inquiry into relationship** between change and power—Generating and Testing Hypotheses Lesson Framework ***What is the relationship between*** *change and power?* **Why** *do people resist the dominant culture or society's rules/laws?* -Return to original thinking -Develop hypotheses about specific context -Explore a specific context to deepen understanding -I used to think . . . but then (with context) . . . so now I think . . . . -Transfer understanding to similar situation	**Metacognition** and **goal-setting** day *Where am I in the learning journey? What do I need to do next?* -Mini-lesson on building metacognition -Return to rubric and exemplar work -Identify areas of strengths and areas for growth -Reflect on strategy to build memory -Compare conceptual learning with traditional learning -Teacher provides feedback based on responses collected from previous lesson

Knowledge drills *How can I build automaticity of key information or skills?* -Mini-lesson on strategies for memorization/automaticity -Quiz on key terms -Academic vocabulary games for culture, subculture, dominant ideology, revolution and innovation -Students record level of recall and compare to previous -Students select strategy to build habit	Expand inquiry into additional concepts of subculture, methods of protest and dominant ideology—Generating and Testing Hypotheses Lesson Framework *What is the relationship between subculture, modes of protest, and dominant ideology?* -Return to previous thinking -Develop hypotheses about new specific context -Explore new specific context to deepen understanding -Partner coaching to deepen understanding	Transfer inquiry into relationships between change, power, subculture, modes of protest, and dominant ideology *How well does my understanding hold up in new situations? What is different about the new situation from previous situations? How does complicating my understanding deepen my understanding?* -Students select from list of new contexts -Compare statements of conceptual relationship to new situation
Investigating: Analyzing historical accounts *How do historians analyze accounts of past events?* -Mini-lesson on evaluating reliability of a source -Application to protest movement -Mini-lesson on inferences based on evidence -Application to protest movement	Communication Skills: Debate *What strategies are necessary for effective debate?* -Mini-lesson on debate strategies -Application to protest movement	Skill Drills *How can I build automaticity of key skills?* -Mini-lesson on strategies for skill automaticity -Quiz on key skills -Students record level of skill ability -Students select strategy to build habit
Metacognition and goal-setting day *Where am I in the learning journey? What do I need to do next?* -Mini-lesson on building metacognition -Return to rubric and exemplar work -ID areas of strengths and areas for growth -Reflect on previous metacognition strategy	Investigating: Formulating an action plan for research *How do I make an action plan for research?* -Mini-lesson on creating an action plan for research -Application to protest movement	Research Day—independent work time -Teacher provides feedback and small group instruction
Summative Assessment	Summative Assessment	Reflection Day *How did I grow intellectually from this unit? How did my understanding of the relationship between change and power deepen? What study skills did I learn? How can I improve as a learner in the next unit?*

SOURCE: Co-created with Neville Kirton, Humanities Department Head, Colegio Anglo Colombiano. Reprinted with permission.

"Polly parrot" learners: "I can't understand anything unless you tell me exactly how and what to say and think. I need you to figure out everything for me. I shouldn't have to do more than repeat what you or the textbook say."

Unfortunately, the more students grow in this direction, the more teachers try to amplify their mother robin teaching to accommodate it. Growth on either side produces a compensating growth on the other. By the Middle School level most students are deeply entrenched in learning, and teachers in teaching, nothing but lower order, fragmented, surface knowledge. Teachers feel by this level that they have no choice but to think for their students, or worse, that they should not require any thinking at all, that students are not really capable of it.

We love this article and suggest reading it in its entirety. It reminds us that our solution to the problem of chronic forgetting—more review, more discrete practice, more work to "break it down" for students—often only makes the problem worse—not to mention the time that is wasted in doing this!

The words of a conceptual teacher:

"Every time I taught this lesson before by explaining it and demonstrating it, a few lessons later students couldn't recall exactly why the elements burned differently. When I taught this lesson conceptually and inductively, the misconceptions were far fewer because they are connecting their observation with the concepts—and can remember what they observed between the concepts on an emotional level." —Julia Briggs, IB Chemistry teacher

Let us say this: Research—and all of our experience—says that if students deeply understand the conceptual relationships of an academic discipline, they will retain facts better and be able to transfer what they've learned (Bransford, 2000; Bruner, 1977; Hattie, 2012; Newmann, Bryk, & Nagaoka, 2001). If they don't deeply understand, they will forget and need it to be repeated again and again, year after year. Most teachers think about their course in isolation. Many do not realize the incredible amount of repetition that happens year after year in almost all of the subject areas, especially language arts and mathematics. In a topic-based, coverage-centered teaching model, the results are plain and simple: Students forget. It's as if they go home at night, lay down, and everything falls out of their ears and onto the floor!

We understand the need for skills practice and memorization to the point of automaticity. Balance is important, and it is wise to spend some time each week developing students' memory and speed at recall of important facts or basic skills. As a general practice, it makes sense to allow time for this *after* we have hooked students with an interesting conceptual question, concept-attainment lessons, and at least one exploration of an abstract conceptual relationship grounded in an interesting context of factual content. Understanding first, drills for automaticity second.

Conclusion

This chapter provides four instructional frameworks to help guide teachers as we experiment with lesson planning for deep, conceptual learning. This is not an exhaustive list of how we can foster students' ability to uncover conceptual relationships and transfer their understanding. No matter what instructional design method you use or your school uses, remember to keep conceptual relationships as the goal as you plan and you will be well on your way.

Chapter Review

- How do conceptual questions help students learn? How do thought-provoking questions help teachers plan?

- How do specific contexts deepen student understanding about conceptual relationships?

- Why is it essential for students to use factual evidence to support their statements of conceptual relationships?

- How might you convince someone that teaching conceptually is worth the time it takes?

....

CHAPTER 5

How Do We Design Assessments for Conceptual Understanding?

Please select the *best* answer to the following question:

Why do we assess students?
   A. To categorize students based on performance
   B. To evaluate students' understanding of a topic or skills
   C. To understand where students are and how we can help them grow
   D. To facilitate students' understanding of their own growth

The right answer is . . . well, it's not that simple. First, our own bias: In our ideal world the answer to this question would always be C and D. We dream of a teaching and learning setting where students are internally motivated to learn, move at a pace that is appropriately challenging, and receive something more like scout badges for demonstration of mastery of skills, rather than numerical scores. We also believe that conceptual understanding is something that doesn't fit into the paradigm of checking objectives off a list as they are mastered. Conceptual understandings should **continuously be refined and deepened** as students grow.

We don't expect that at the end of a unit on, say, the California Gold Rush, students will understand all the dimensions of the relationship between power and natural resources. Instead, our hope is that students are inspired to continue looking for connections between examples that will push and enrich their understanding. That means that assessment isn't about "mastery" as much as it is about dialogue and feedback. We'd rather help students reflect on their learning and continuously grow than say "B+." That's the dream.

Now onto the reality. Having worked in schools across the world and education spectrum, we know that assessment is a tricky and loaded topic—the spark of countless heated debates (we've been in many!). We know that each of you reading this book likely lives in a different ecosystem of evaluating student progress. For some of you the state test might be the be-all-end-all of your school's vision of assessment. Others might be pushing your colleagues to experiment with dialogical assessment, abandon traditional grades, and focus on student reflection. Our hope is that this chapter will support you in making meaning of and measuring student progress toward worthwhile goals in an authentic way, regardless of where you find yourselves on that spectrum.

In this chapter we'll provide several principles for designing your own system of assessment along with many practical examples that will help you see what it looks like to assess conceptual understanding. Every school and often every teacher has their own unique way of recording student scores. Our approach aims to value your particular circumstances as well as encourage innovation.

Two Quick Caveats

- We are not experts in testing, especially about when and how to assign scores or grades (psychometrics is not our specialty). Instead we offer ideas and insights that come from working with students and teachers in classrooms to find systems for assessment that are useful and meaningful to their work.

- The whole enterprise of assessment is fraught with questions of legitimacy and fairness. Too often assessments are used to divide students into categories and too often demographic factors predict assessment outcomes. The relationship between assessment and equity is a complex issue that deserves its own book. That's not to say we won't acknowledge this reality in this chapter.

Four Principles for Assessment in a Concept-Based Classroom

1. **Transfer is the ultimate goal.** As conceptual learning guru Lois Lanning (2009) wrote, "The most important skills, knowledge, attitudes, and understandings that students acquire through schools are relevant because they have value and application in later times and in different circumstances" (p. 13). We ultimately want students to use their conceptual understanding to understand and transform their world. That means these understandings cannot be inert knowledge but rather keys to unlocking new situations. If that is our goal, our assessments need to provide insight on our progress toward students transferring their understanding to new situations.

2. **Mistakes are important.** Stumbles and missteps are expected, valued, and made meaningful. We must provide opportunities for students to *safely and nonpunitively* test their initial understandings, notice what needs improvement, and continue working until they get to a satisfactory level.

3. **It's not about right or wrong—it's about progress and evidence.** Students are often trained to look for the right answer. With assessment for conceptual understanding, we need to shift their questions from "Is this right?" to "Does my evidence/example support my understanding?" and "How can I deepen my understanding of these ideas?" We want students to continuously push their own growth and see their efforts on a spectrum from a simplistic to sophisticated understanding of concepts fueled by evidence. Learning best happens in a culture of *continuous growth.*

4. **Provide feedback throughout—not just at the end.** Students need constructive feedback that they can use to improve throughout their exploration of a concept. Rather than waiting until the end of a unit to provide students with feedback, there needs to be constant conversation with teachers and peers about how they can deepen their understanding. Rather than giving students a detailed autopsy of their understanding once we've moved on, provide them with frequent feedback on their progress along the way.

In practice, these principles translate into a classroom where teachers constantly collect nonpunitive evidence of student understanding. Students collect evidence of and set their own goals for improving their level of understanding. Students also receive feedback that helps them figure out what to do next.

For example, imagine you were exploring the relationship between surface area and volume. You might create an assessment plan like the one outlined in Figure 5.1.

Throughout the unit the teacher is always gathering information about where students are and using that information to provide feedback and make adjustments. Figure 5.1 lays out a wholesale shift in assessment toward the Concept-Based approach. It is not necessary, however, as you begin to experiment with this type of assessment that you shift all your assessment to this model. Instead start by trying out the principles discussed earlier in small ways and seeing what works for your students in your context. We have no doubt that if you align with the principles and continuously reflect on your progress you'll make great strides toward assessment that supports conceptual learning. We're excited to hear from our readers about the innovative ideas for assessment you develop! Throughout this chapter you'll see examples from our practice (in Grades 6–12) over the years. See Figure 5.2 for an example of formative assessment in a unit.

You'll notice that in our examples, assessment does not come only at the end of the unit but frequently throughout. This is the major difference between *formative* assessment and *summative* assessment. Formative assessment happens throughout a unit and should be used to help students form their understanding of both the conceptual relationships as well as of how they learn. This type of feedback helps students push their thinking, get on the right track, and make sense of errors along the way.

FIGURE 5.1   ASSESSMENT OVERVIEW

When?	Assessment Step	Examples
At the beginning of the unit	Preassess understanding of individual concepts	**Define surface area in your own words.** **Define volume in your own words.** *Provide feedback on any misconceptions or shallow understandings.*
After a few lessons	Measure *initial* understanding of conceptual relationships	**What is the relationship between surface area and volume? Use evidence from your experiments and problem solving to support your answer.** *Allow students to access notes from group work, class discussions, and experiments as well as any common texts.*
Throughout the unit	Measure *deepening and refining* of understanding of conceptual relationships	*Repeat the question above, asking students to incorporate additional examples from your exploration in class and use the rubric to evaluate where they are at this moment. Also ask them to think of ways to improve.*
At least once before the summative assessment	Measure ability to *transfer* understanding of conceptual relationships	*Provide students with several inputs (articles, examples, experiments, etc.) about a new situation (an origami inquiry) and ask the following:* **How does this information clarify, contradict, or confirm your understanding of surface area and volume?**
End of unit (summative assessment)	Measure *transfer* and *depth* of understanding of conceptual relationships	*Provide students with several inputs (articles, examples, experiments, etc.) about a new situation (in this case, a bottling company trying to minimize packaging and maximize volume) and ask the following:* **Based on your understanding of surface area and volume, and given the constraints of our company, how should we design our packaging?**
End of unit (reflection)	Measure metacognitive awareness of understanding and growth	*Ask students to assess their own understanding using the rubric.* **Write a reflection about where your understanding falls on the rubric, defend why it falls there with evidence, and explain how your thinking progressed throughout the unit.** *The teacher reads each reflection and writes back to students with feedback on strengths and areas for growth as well as the teacher's assessment of where each student's understanding falls on the rubric. That assessment could include a note that there is a disconnection between what is written and what the teacher observed in the student's understanding. This conversation could also happen verbally.*

FIGURE 5.2   USING A FORMATIVE ASSESSMENT EXAMPLE

Throughout the unit, a teacher jots down notes on his clipboard (or maybe iPad) about where each student is in his or her understanding of these concepts. Maybe he marks on a rubric or just writes down a few key words to help him remember where that student is in his or her thinking. The teacher especially notes any misconceptions he hears from students so he can tackle those directly.

In one lesson, students are given several rectangular prisms (boxes) of various sizes. Their task is to explore the relationship between the surface area and volume of each box. The day after that experiment, the teacher asks students to write their understanding of the relationship between surface area and volume along with evidence that supports that understanding. He then has his students do a gallery walk where they provide feedback to one another about their understandings. Students leave sticky notes with warm and cool feedback for their peers. Students have an opportunity to revise their understandings based on this feedback. After class, the teacher uses the information he gathers to design the next experiment that students will do to explore volume and surface area. He noticed many students understand that *to increase volume, the surface area of an object must also increase*, so their experiment tomorrow will focus on that element of the relationship between the concepts.

Next, the teacher challenges students to design 3-D figures with the same surface area but different volumes, which challenges their previous understanding that *to increase volume, the surface area of an object must also increase*. Now they see that the compactness of a 3-D shape also plays a role in the relationship between surface area and volume. The teacher asks students to revise their understanding of the relationship between the concepts in light of this new learning. He then asks each student to assess their own revised understanding using a rubric they have employed several times this year. After class, the teacher reviews each student's understanding and his or her reflection on that understanding. He prepares to conference with students the next day by planning what feedback he will provide and what questions he will ask to push students' thinking.

When students receive formative assessment, they have opportunities to improve. The assessment is valuable because students are still working toward their final goal. In addition, formative assessment provides information to help the teacher adjust his or her instruction. For example, if you notice during formative assessment that many students have the same misunderstanding, you may choose to directly address that misunderstanding through a lesson or learning experience. In short, the goal of formative assessment is to provide opportunities for both students and teachers to reflect on progress and adjust, revise, or refine their work.

Conversely, summative assessment occurs at the *end point* in the learning journey, most often at the end of a unit or semester. The purpose of summative assessment is traditionally evaluation—to measure whether the student reached the goal and, if not, how far off from the goal he or she was. That evaluation often takes the form of letter grades (B = close to the goal, but not there yet) or numbers out of 100 (60 = very far from the goal). There are so many important reasons why summative assessment matters. For example, many teachers need to give a traditional grade at the end of the unit, whether because of school policy or simply because students need grades for their transcripts in order to pursue higher education.

We would argue that this assessment is—in terms of teaching and learning— far less important than formative assessment. How many times have you seen a student get a test or paper back with a grade and crumple it up either out of frustration or indifference? Our experience and research (Brookhart, 2008) shows that when there is a grade on an assignment, students will simply look at the letter or number and disregard the substantive comments. The information that is most important to learning is the feedback that students can use to improve their work. While summative assessment often gets all the attention, it's formative assessment that can do the important work. See also Figure 5.3 for a brief point about standardized tests.

FIGURE 5.3 THE STANDARDIZED TEST QUESTION

For many of you, this chapter will bring up questions (and maybe a bit of anxiety) about how conceptual teaching and learning will affect students' performance on standardized tests. While there's a lot we could say on this topic, here is one important point:

We do not need to decide between students doing meaningful intellectual work (the type of work that happens in a Concept-Based classroom) and basic skills development. Newmann et al. wrote the following in their 2001 study, *Authentic Intellectual Work and Standardized Tests: Conflict or Coexistence?*:

> Discussion of best instructional practices or forms of assessment ... frequently poses a dichotomy between teaching approaches that enhance basic skills versus those that aim at more ambitious intellectual work, implying a trade-off between these two educational goals. The evidence presented here suggests that this debate rests on a false dichotomy. (p. 2)

You cannot deepen your understanding of the relationship between population and energy without effectively reading complex texts like a scientific journal article about grey wolf populations in national parks. Developing complex and sophisticated conceptual understanding is intricately linked with developing basic skills—and makes that work so much more meaningful for students. And as we know, when we make work meaningful, it's more likely to stick! Long story (and lots of research) short— students *can* develop basic skills in service of a more authentic purpose.

For more on the relationship between concepts and the Common Core State Standards, please see Chapter 7.

Tips for Summative Assessment

While the focus of this chapter is assessment for learning (formative assessment), we recognize the importance of summative assessment, especially in connection to grading. Below are a few tips to follow when it's time for summative assessment.

- All the rubrics described throughout this chapter can also be used for summative assessment. In fact, when teachers use the same rubrics for summative assessment as they have used for formative assessment, the goals are clearer to students. Instead of trying to figure out what is expected, students have a clear idea of their ultimate aim. The context needs to be novel so they aren't simply recalling and regurgitating information they have previously discussed in class.

- The question formats and structures for assessment described throughout this chapter can also be used for summative assessment. While the exact content of the questions should vary so students do not see the same questions they have seen before, the design principles remain the same. The one exception is that it is valuable to always ask students to describe relationships between concepts—a question they should have seen throughout their formative assessment—on their summative assessment. Students should be given novel facts or a new situation to stretch their understanding, but the question of "What is the relationship between X concept and Y concept?" can remain the same.

- Consider summative assessment and grading that focus on growth rather than absolute levels. Student portfolios, one structure that can be used for this, are described in Figure 5.19. Grading based on growth motivates both students who are struggling (and might be disengaged by a perception of not being able to succeed) and those who are excelling (and need a challenge to push them beyond the standard expectation). Grading for growth, therefore, can create differentiation and motivation for students.

Designing Formative Assessments

Not all formative assessments, however, are created equal. Formative assessment is only as good as the information it gives teachers and students about where they are and where they need to go. To do the important work of pushing students' thinking and deepening their conceptual understanding, formative assessment must do two things:

1. Make students' current thinking about the conceptual relationship visible

2. Leverage effective feedback to push student thinking forward

To make students' thinking visible, formative assessments must be carefully designed. It is easy to mistakenly assess students' ability to recall facts learned in class rather than ask students to generate their own understanding of the relationship between concepts. In Chapter 1, we discussed Anderson and Krathwohl's (2001) revision of Bloom's taxonomy and the addition of the knowledge dimension. For a moment, though, we'll return to the cognitive processes: remember, understand, apply, analyze, evaluate, and create (see Figure 5.4).

FIGURE 5.4   REVISED BLOOM'S TAXONOMY

Knowledge Dimension	Cognitive Process Dimension					
	Remember	Understand	Apply	Analyze	Evaluate	Create
Factual Knowledge						
Conceptual Knowledge						
Procedural Knowledge						
Metacognitive Knowledge						

SOURCE: Anderson & Krathwohl (2001).

When we are assessing conceptual understanding, we need to avoid mistaking students' ability to remember facts for their having a deep and complex understanding of concepts. For example, if we ask students to discuss what they have learned within a context they are already familiar with, often they can easily regurgitate what we have covered in class. It's sometimes tempting to go through this process and hear students parrot back to us our own thinking. If we do this, however, we are not actually assessing students' understanding, just their ability to recall information they have already learned.

Strategy #1: Use Novel Information

To truly assess students' understanding, or any other higher thinking process, it is critical that we ask them to transfer their understanding to a novel situation. See Figure 5.5 for an example.

As stated in Chapter 1, Perkins and Salomon (1988) referred to this as "high-road transfer," meaning it is not simply applying the same rote procedure in a new situation. Instead, we are asking students to build their understanding, abstract the relationship between concepts, and return that understanding to a new factual situation.

FIGURE 5.5 TRANSFER EXAMPLE

What does this look like?

Imagine your students are exploring the relationship between environment and evolution. If in class you discussed this conceptual relationship in the context of Ice Age adaptations, for the assessment you might ask students to show their understanding of this same relationship in the context of modern pollution. Initially, this way of assessing might feel uncomfortable to both you and your students. We've heard teachers and students say, "But we didn't learn this."

Our answer is, "Yes, exactly, you didn't learn it, but you can figure it out!" The goal is for students to apply and stretch their understanding with a new factual context. In this example, you will avoid mistaking students' ability to remember facts about the Ice Age for true understanding. Instead, you'll be able to assess how well students are able to *transfer* their understanding of evolution and the environment to a new situation. The ideas are the same, but the facts are different. Providing different facts allows student thinking about the conceptual relationship to become visible.

FIGURE 5.6 VISIBLE LEARNING FOR LITERACY

Hugging to Promote Low-Road Transfer _Students are learning to apply skills and knowledge._	Bridging to Promote High-Road Transfer _Students are learning to make links across concepts._
Teacher is associating prior knowledge with new knowledge. Students are categorizing information. The teacher is modeling and thinking aloud. Students are summarizing and rehearsing knowledge. The teacher creates role-play and simulation opportunities for students to apply new knowledge to parallel situations.	Students are using analogies and metaphors to illustrate connections across disciplines or content. Students are deriving rules and principles based on examples. Students are thinking metacognitively and reflectively to plan and organize. Students are creating new and original content. Students are applying new knowledge to dissimilar situations.

SOURCE: Fisher, D., Frey, N., & Hattie, J. (2016).

Students use their conceptual understanding as a lens to interpret the new situation, and that situation in turn refines their lens. Figure 5.6 above illustrates different methods for different types of transfer. Notice the bottom right box where students apply new knowledge to *dissimilar situations.*

This same principle is evident in Brookhart's (2010) guidelines for assessing higher order thinking. Brookhart advises assessment designers to present something for students to think about and to use novel material. Again these guidelines help us—as assessment designers—to narrow in on what we actually hope to evaluate: students thinking about concepts. If we don't give students something to think about (text, a video, an image), we are expecting them to draw from their memory and therefore assessing at least partially their ability to recall information. Similarly, if the material we provide isn't novel, students can rely on their memories rather than having to apply their conceptual understanding. To truly assess students' conceptual understanding, we need to ask them to apply that understanding to situations they have not yet seen.

> To truly assess students' conceptual understanding, we need to ask them to apply that understanding to situations they have not yet seen.

Strategy #2: Vary the Assessment Method

While the principles of assessment for conceptual learning outlined earlier should remain the same, the exact form of assessments can vary significantly. For example, early in the unit, rather than asking students to define concepts, students could select the best example of a particular concept from a variety of examples. This assessment could be multiple choice (see Figure 5.7) or matching (see Figure 5.8).

FIGURE 5.7 MULTIPLE-CHOICE EXAMPLE

Read the following excerpt from Zora Neale Hurston's *Their Eyes Were Watching God.*

The people all saw her come because it was sundown. The sun was gone, but he had left his footprints in the sky. It was the time for sitting on porches beside the road. It was the time to hear things and talk. These sitters had been tongueless, earless, eyeless conveniences all day long. Mules and other brutes had occupied their skins. But now, the sun and the bossman were gone, so the skins felt powerful and human. They became lords of sounds and lesser things. They passed nations through their mouths. They sat in judgment.

Which of the following is an example of personification?

A. The people all saw her come because it was sundown.

B. The sun was gone, but he had left his footprints in the sky.

C. These sitters had been tongueless, earless, eyeless conveniences all day long.

D. They became lords of sounds and lesser things.

FIGURE 5.8 MATCHING EXAMPLE

For questions 1 to 4, match the concept with the scenario that is the best example of the concept.	
1. Globalization	A. The cost of producing goods is cheaper in China than it is in the United States.
2. Outsourcing	B. Europe's economy is in crisis, which negatively affects the U.S. economy because we rely on Europe for goods.
3. Comparative Advantage	C. Jobs like phone operators for most U.S. companies are now based in India instead of the United States.
4. Economic Interdependence	D. McDonald's was formed in the United States but now exists in almost every country in the world.

While these types of questions will give you some insight into students' understanding, it can be difficult to determine why they chose the answer they did (right or wrong). One possible way to deepen your understanding of their thinking is to ask students to explain their reasoning. After completing a selected response like these, students could explain why they chose their selected answer. In Figure 5.7, for example, a student might select option C as an example of personification. The choice may baffle the teacher at first. If, however, a teacher asks his or her students to explain their reasoning, the teacher might learn that the student categorized option C as personification either because it referred to parts of living things or because it was a metaphor—two very different misconceptions! This type of question can help teachers uncover the "why" behind incorrect answers.

Of course, selected-response or open-ended questions are not the only ways to gauge student understanding. When you begin assessing students' understanding of the relationship between concepts, students could draw or explain verbally the relationship rather than writing a constructed response. You could even assess students' understanding of concepts, ability to defend their understanding with evidence, and capacity to transfer that understanding to a new situation through a Socratic Seminar (see page 106, Figure 5.9). In a Socratic seminar, students could have a text-based, student-driven discussion of either more theoretical questions such as "What is the relationship between power and resources?" or more context-based questions that ask students to apply their conceptual understanding to unlock a new situation. For example, a driving question for the Socratic seminar could be, "Is the death penalty just?" Students could then apply their understanding of the relationship between justice and consequences along with various articles on that issue.

FIGURE 5.9   SOCRATIC SEMINAR TRACKER

Socratic Seminar Tracker												
Student Name	Conceptual Understanding				Evidence to Support Understanding				Transfer			
Student 1	1	2	3	4	1	2	3	4	1	2	3	4
Student 2	1	2	3	4	1	2	3	4	1	2	3	4
Student 3	1	2	3	4	1	2	3	4	1	2	3	4
Student 4	1	2	3	4	1	2	3	4	1	2	3	4
Student 5	1	2	3	4	1	2	3	4	1	2	3	4

Track student understanding of concepts in a Socratic seminar using this chart and an accompanying rubric (rubric examples follow). In addition to noting the level of students' conceptual understanding, ability to use evidence, and capacity to transfer their understanding to a new situation, jot down notes on this chart to help you provide effective feedback to students after the discussion. With proper scaffolding, students can even track one another's understanding in a fishbowl-style conversation.

Examples and Nonexamples of Effective Conceptual Assessments

The key with any assessment is to ensure that student thinking about the concepts is visible. The same is true when students transfer their understanding to a new issue or question—you need to be able to see how they are using the conceptual relationship to unlock a novel situation. To help clarify these ideas, the following are a few examples of effective conceptual assessments as well as a few nonexamples. Take a moment to categorize them by figuring out which are examples of the types of assessments we have been discussing and which are nonexamples (see Figures 5.10, 5.11, and 5.12).

FIGURE 5.10   CONCEPTUAL VERSUS FACTUAL EXAMPLE 1

1. What year was *Their Eyes Were Watching God* published?

A. 1997

B. 1838

C. 1937

D. 1871

FIGURE 5.11 CONCEPTUAL VERSUS FACTUAL EXAMPLE 2

1. What statement best describes Bigger's point of view in the passage below?

   "I don't know. I just feel that way. Every time I get to thinking about me being black and they being white, me being here and they being there, I feel like something awful's going to happen to me. . . ."

   A. He is afraid of something bad happening to him.

   B. He believes he won't be able to continue to function within the rules of an unjust system.

   C. He dislikes the racial inequality in America and is committed to fighting against it.

   D. He is worried about the safety of his friends.

Figure 5.12 assesses conceptual understanding. The reaction described is an example of a synthesis reaction. The question asks students to correctly classify a particular case within a conceptual category. Figure 5.10 assesses factual information. It simply asks students to remember the year of publication. There is nothing to figure out or think through. They must rely on their ability to recall information—often facts to answer the question. Figure 5.11 assesses reading comprehension. Though "point of view" is a concept, all of the possible answer choices could be a point of view, so students are not chiefly being assessed on their understanding of point of view. Instead they are being assessed on their ability to understand a particular character's point of view. Understanding the concept of point of view is helpful and indeed necessary to answer this question correctly, but it is not the primary focus.

FIGURE 5.12 CONCEPTUAL VERSUS FACTUAL EXAMPLE 3

How is this reaction classified?

$$CaO + H_2O = Ca(OH)_2 + heat$$

A. synthesis

B. single replacement

C. decomposition

D. double replacement

The Power of Effective Feedback

Teacher feedback on student work can be a powerful tool to dramatically improve student learning. However, the *quality* of the feedback is essential—low-quality feedback can actually have negative effects on student growth. Feedback cannot simply say, "You are not at the learning goal yet." It should indicate exactly where on the learning journey a student is and which habits or strategies the student is using that might be working or might need to be changed and give the student ideas for what to do next. It must demonstrate a belief in students' capacity to reach the goal even while providing specific growth areas. To be effective, feedback must also be well-timed to help push a student's thinking to the next level. As Brookhart (2008) explained in her book, *How to Give Effective Feedback to Your Students,* "Feedback . . . is just-in-time, just-for-me information delivered when and where it can do the most good" (p. 1).

Strategy #3: Use Effective Feedback

1. Start with a clear goal. (See the discussion of rubrics and models later.)

2. Describe the student's current work in relation to the overall goal. Focus on being descriptive rather than evaluative.

3. Think about the feedback from the student's perspective. What would you want to hear?

4. Help the student figure out what to do next, but don't provide the answer or make all the corrections for the student.

5. Be encouraging and specific.

See Figure 5.13 for a few examples of effective feedback.

FIGURE 5.13   SAMPLE FEEDBACK

Sample Feedback	Thoughts on the Feedback
"Your conceptual understanding describes the relationship between two or more concepts. Your explanation is clear and demonstrates you have a deep understanding of the relationship. The example that supports your statement about the concept isn't relevant. What other examples can you think of that relate to the relationship you describe?"	*This feedback is focused on the goal of conceptual understanding and gives specific instructions on what is missing. It is also descriptive and not evaluative. It moves the student forward in his or her thinking without providing an answer.*
"You used a lot of examples to support your statement of conceptual relationship. That makes your statement really compelling. How did you think of examples we had not talked about in class?"	*This feedback is positive and descriptive. It is likely for a student who may have been previously struggling with producing examples outside of class. The question allows the student to reflect on how he or she achieved this so as to continue on this path toward success.*

Sample Feedback	Thoughts on the Feedback
"Your statement is complex and precise. The examples clearly support the relationship between the concepts in the statement. How might you increase the sophistication of the conceptual relationship to make it even more profound?"	*This is descriptive, positive feedback for a student who is well on track for the learning target. The question gives this student something to work on for improvement, promoting a culture of continuous growth.*

Berger (2003) suggested that feedback—or critique, as he referred to it—should be kind, helpful, and specific. These straightforward and simple guidelines help both teachers and students provide feedback to one another. Remember, the teacher does not need to be the only person providing feedback. Students can review one another's work and share ideas for improvement. In addition, students can reflect on their own work and, with the help of models and rubrics, self-assess.

Why Models Matter

What makes Leonardo da Vinci's *Mona Lisa* an exceptional piece of art? Imagine you were teaching a class and trying to describe the qualities of the *Mona Lisa* without showing the painting to your students. Everyone would think you were nuts. The descriptors without the work itself would fall flat. This seems like an extreme example, but in education we do it all the time. Too often we ask students to create something without showing them an example of a high-quality final product. Sharing a model—whether student work or something we create—is powerful in both motivating students (they see what is possible) and guiding them toward the goal (instead of an abstract idea, they have a concrete example).

Strategy #4: Use Models to Help Demonstrate Conceptual Understanding

In the world of conceptual teaching and learning, this means we need to show students models of complex, insightful generalizations supported by compelling, sufficient evidence. We want these models to inspire students and make them think, "I can create something as profound and well-defended as that!" Models should be intellectual candy for students. Of course, they cannot be the exact "answer" you are looking for. Your example shouldn't be about the conceptual relationship you are exploring; that makes it seem like there is one right answer and you just showed the students the back of the book. Instead, share examples of different conceptual relationships and have students analyze what makes those examples so high quality. Why is one generalization better than another? Let students figure it out and name the qualities. Show students the *Mona Lisa, The Last Supper,* and *The Adoration of the Magi* and let them describe what qualities make these works so compelling.

More Ways to Use Models/Examples

- *Show students weaker models and as a class ask them to improve those examples to make them more sophisticated.* Ask students to provide feedback to help improve a weak generalization. Not only does this support them in internalizing the questions to ask themselves as they are developing their own understanding of concepts, but it also sets students up for providing high-quality feedback to their peers.

- *Share one student's generalization and work together to make it stronger as a class.* When you start with actually looking at the work, you ground yourself and students in a strong foundation for understanding what the goal is and how to get there. Create a community in your classroom where students are comfortable sharing their unfinished work with one another.

- *Share examples/models of effective peer feedback.* This will help students develop their ability to provide one another with support in deepening their understanding. Consider sharing sentence stems or questions students could use to push one another's thinking.

The Promise of Rubrics

Let's be honest: It's more difficult to assess deep conceptual understanding than it is to assess simple recall. Rather than simply determining whether students got the answer right or wrong, assessing conceptual understanding requires evaluating where students' generalization falls on a spectrum of accuracy, adequate support, and sophistication. Rubrics can be a helpful tool in both outlining this spectrum for students and providing descriptive feedback in a way that is both efficient and effective. A descriptive and clear rubric can transform learning by providing students with information about where they are and what they need to do to grow.

For example, a rubric that explains the spectrum of conceptual understanding would let students know that the essential criteria for conceptual understandings are:

- Articulation and explanation of a conceptual relationship in students' own words
- Factual examples to support their articulation and explanation

Once students reach this level with their work, they could look at the description for advanced conceptual understanding and see that their generalization should include:

- Analysis and synthesis of the conceptual statement in connection to multiple examples
- Evaluation of the transferability of the conceptual statement

These descriptors will not be meaningful to students unless they've seen work samples at each of these different levels. Students must internalize and practice with the rubric well before any formal scoring takes place. In education, we often talk about teachers norming with rubrics. This means that they collaboratively use the rubric with sample work to determine if they have a shared understanding of the rubric that they can use to assess student work. Teachers calibrate with one another to make sure their evaluations of different student work examples are fairly aligned. For rubrics to be effective tools in providing meaningful feedback, students must also understand what each descriptor means and have a picture of what work looks like at the different levels. Just as teachers need to norm with rubrics, students need to calibrate their understanding of the rubric with work samples. Rubrics will never be able to be both clear and concise enough to be meaningful unless they are accompanied by illustrative work samples that bring the rubric descriptors to life.

Strategy #5: Use Rubrics to Further Demonstrate a Range of Conceptual Understanding

We find that with strong work samples, rubrics can be very simple. For example, Figure 5.14 is a sample rubric for early middle school. In the column below the description of each level is a sample student generalization that illuminates the meaning of the rubric description.

FIGURE 5.14   RUBRIC EXAMPLE 1

1	2	3
I can explain the concepts in my own words and give an example of each.	I can explain a weak relationship between two concepts in my own words and give an accurate and relevant example.	I can explain a strong relationship between two concepts in my own words and provide powerful, clear examples that prove that relationship.
Humans are living things that can talk. For example, I am a human. Resources are things that we can use for different reasons. For example, water is a resource.	*Human beings use resources. For example, people in my town use water to keep their lawns green and to bathe.*	*Human beings rely on resources in order to survive. For example, without water, humans die in a matter of days. Additionally, humans use natural resources to make the shelters they need to survive. Without shelters, humans will die from exposure.*

Notice how the rubric begins at the level where students are not describing the relationship between the concepts but only each individual concept on its own. The next level of progression is a student identifying a simplistic (and often obvious) relationship between the concepts. Frequently students can achieve this level without a lot of in-depth study of the concepts. By the third level, students are describing a more sophisticated relationship between the concepts. This relationship is normally more specific than the simplistic relationship (e.g., *humans use resources* vs. *humans rely on resources for survival*). This more sophisticated generalization is drawn from student analysis of examples and abstracting from several different contexts.

Along the way students might write generalizations that don't exactly match any of these levels. Perhaps their generalization is sophisticated but supported with inaccurate examples. Perhaps their examples are relevant to one of the concepts, but they don't illustrate the *relationship* between the concepts in a compelling way. Even in these outlier examples, having the rubric still helps both teachers and students unpack where they are and think about what to do next. If the generalization is simplistic, students can ask themselves why the relationship exists, why it's important, or how the concepts influence one another. If the examples are irrelevant, students can find more meaningful support for their generalization.

This same framework applies when the rubric itself becomes more sophisticated. Take a look at the simple rubric in Figure 5.15 for conceptual understanding at the high school level. The rubric describes different possible levels of students' ability to explain the relationship between concepts and differentiates between what students can do independently and what they can do with support (peer or teacher coaching).

FIGURE 5.15   RUBRIC EXAMPLE 2

	OFF TRACK (0)	NOVICE (1–2)	APPRENTICE (3–4)	PRACTITIONER (5–6)	EXPERT (7–8)
Conceptual Understanding	Even with help, I cannot state, explain, and provide an example of a simplistic relationship between the concepts.	I can state a simplistic and vague relationship between the concepts. *I need help to explain and give examples of my idea. (In other words . . . For example . . .)*	I can state, explain, and give examples of a simplistic relationship between the concepts. *I need help to make my idea complex and precise. (How or why?)*	I can state, explain, and give examples of a complex and precise relationship between the concepts. *I need help to make my idea significant. (So what?)*	I can state, explain, and give examples of a complex, precise, and significant relationship between the concepts. *I can help others make their ideas more complex, precise, and significant.*

Now that you've had a chance to work with a few simpler rubrics, try using the more complex version shown in Figure 5.16. This advanced rubric disaggregates the conceptual understanding, analysis, and transferability of the conceptual relationship statement and therefore allows the feedback to be more targeted. You might use a rubric

FIGURE 5.16   RUBRIC EXAMPLE 3

	OFF TRACK	NOVICE	APPRENTICE	PRACTITIONER	EXPERT
Overall	My understanding of the concepts is **inaccurate.**	My understanding of the concepts is **partial.**	My understanding of the concepts is **fully developed.**	My understanding of the concepts is **complex.**	My understanding of the concepts is **precise, complex, significant,** and **transferable.**
Conceptual Understanding	Generalizations show **misunderstandings** or confusion. Examples are used inappropriately or not at all.	Generalizations are **vague** or **simplistic.** Few examples are used to illustrate ideas.	Generalizations state a **complete, precise** relationship. **Sufficient** examples are used to illustrate ideas.	Generalizations are **complex** or **sophisticated.** **Relevant, significant** examples are used to **justify** ideas.	Generalizations are complex, precise, and **significant.** **Powerful** examples are used compellingly justify ideas.
Conceptual Analysis and Synthesis	I do not understand how new information relates to my ideas about the concepts.	I **partially** understand how new information confirms, complicates, or contradicts my ideas about the concepts.	I **fully** understand how new information confirms, complicates, or contradicts my ideas about the concepts.	I understand the **complexities** or **nuances** of how new information confirms, complicates, or contradicts my ideas about the concepts.	I understand the **complexities** and **nuances** of how new information relates to my ideas AND can judge how **significant** the new information is to my understanding.
Conceptual Transfer	I do not use my understanding of the concepts to respond to the novel situation OR I use concepts inaccurately.	I use my understanding of **individual concepts** (not the relationship between concepts) to respond to the novel situation.	I use my understanding of the **relationship** between concepts **implicitly** to respond to the novel situation.	I use my understanding of the relationship between concepts **explicitly** and **appropriately** to respond to the novel situation.	I explicitly **evaluate the transferability** of my understanding of the relationship between concepts to the novel situation and **account for nuanced differences** in my response.

like this one to evaluate a student's response to an assessment question, such as, *Based on your understanding of volume and area, how should we redesign the packaging for our company?*

Student Self-Assessment and Goal Setting

Rubrics are not only helpful tools for teachers. The more students are aware of the end goal of their learning and the process of getting there, the more intrinsically motivated they become. When students are able to evaluate their own work against a set of clear criteria, they are empowered to take more control over their learning and decide what to do next. Asking them to set their own short- and long-term goals related to their learning is an additional powerful strategy to boost intrinsic motivation and inspire young people to sit in the driver's seat of their own growth.

In addition, self-assessment and peer assessment can be valuable tools for increasing the amount of feedback students receive in a way that is sustainable for teachers. If you, as a secondary teacher, are seeing 150 students (or more) per day, it can be challenging to provide the personalized feedback that will ignite student growth. While feedback from teachers is important, creating structures and empowering students to provide feedback to themselves and one another not only builds students' capacity as self-directed learners but also creates an ecosystem of feedback. Instead of the teacher being the sole source of guidance, students can push each other and themselves to grow and improve. Not only will building the skills of self-assessment and peer assessment help students grow in your particular class, but it will help them continue to grow for the rest of their lives.

Strategy #6: Set Student Goals

One strategy that can be particularly motivating for students is setting their own goals and tracking progress. Given a rubric and exemplars, students can see where they are, where they are going, and what the steps might be to get there. For example, if at the beginning of the unit students write their initial understanding of a conceptual relationship, they could first assess their sophistication using a rubric and then set a goal for growth. In Figure 5.17, a student has chosen the goal of reaching Practitioner on the rubric. After setting that goal, the student could track his or her progress throughout the unit using a format like the one shown in Figure 5.17.

Strategy #7: Reflect on Student Progress

In addition to tracking their overall growth throughout the unit, students can also regularly reflect on where they are on the rubric using a format like the one in Figure 5.18. This structure asks students not only to self-assess where they are

FIGURE 5.17   STUDENT GOAL-SETTING EXAMPLE

Sample Student Goal-Setting Strategy

Throughout the unit, have students consistently reflect in the same notebook. At the beginning of the unit, ask them to set their goals for what level of understanding they want to reach. Glue, tape, or staple their goal to the inside of their notebook and periodically remind students to track their progress.

My Goal: I can state, explain, and give examples of a complex and precise relationship between the concepts (*Practitioner on the rubric*).

Tracking My Growth:

September 15	Novice (I need to work on finding examples that support my understanding.)
September 28	Apprentice (I need to make my generalization more complex.)
October 5	Novice (I tried to make my generalization more complex, but I got confused with examples.)
October 18	Apprentice (I'm almost at Practitioner. I just need to choose more significant examples to justify my generalization.).

FIGURE 5.18   SAMPLE STUDENT REFLECTION FORM

Sample Student Reflection Form

Reread your explanation of the relationship between **environment** and **evolution**. What level of the rubric describes your answer? (*Circle Below*)

Off-Track   Novice   Apprentice   Practitioner   Expert

Explain why your answer matches the level you circled above. Use evidence from your explanation to prove it.

_____
_____
_____
_____
_____
_____
_____
_____
_____
_____

on the rubric but to use evidence from their answer to defend their evaluation. While this helps students accurately track their own growth, it also builds their automaticity in regularly assessing their own work. Beyond supporting students in developing the sophistication of their understanding of conceptual relationships, this system also helps students develop the habit of critiquing their own work and improving it.

Strategy #8: Use Student Portfolios

Student self-assessment and goal setting can even be used for summative assessment. Figure 5.19 provides an example of a portfolio system for grading. At the end of a unit, the summative assessment could involve students gathering a portfolio of their work that demonstrates their understanding of the conceptual relationship. The portfolio would contain various artifacts that show a student's understanding. Depending on the course, these work products could range from a more traditional essay, to a lab report, to a video of students discussing the topic or even a mathematical proof. In the accompanying narrative, the student could explain and defend how the work product demonstrates that he or she has reached a particular level of understanding about the concepts.

FIGURE 5.19   STUDENT PORTFOLIO EXAMPLE

Using Portfolios

Students can also track their growth over time—within a given conceptual understanding and across their trajectory as a conceptual learner—using portfolios. Over time, students can collect examples of work they are proud of to share either with their teacher, parents, or a panel of outside experts. Work samples can be used to defend the presenting student's overall claims about his or her growth over time.

Sample Portfolio Table of Contents

A. September and June Generalizations—This work sample shows where I was in my ability to write and justify complex conceptual generalizations at the beginning of the year compared to now.

B. Sample Socratic Seminar Rubric—This rubric shows my peers' notes about my participation in a May Socratic seminar. You can see I am consistently reaching the practitioner level with my participation in this seminar.

C. Lab Report—This report shows how I was able to transfer my understanding about the relationship between matter and heat to accurately predict the outcome of a new experiment.

Self-assessment and goal setting take time to learn how to do well. As we discussed earlier, students must understand and internalize the criteria to both set goals and evaluate their progress. Using the same criteria (and even the same rubric) throughout the year and over multiple years to support students as they explore different conceptual relationships can be incredibly valuable. Even when assessing, the criteria that student work is being evaluated against shouldn't be secret. Provide them with access to the rubric before, during, and after the assessment. Students can practice with the rubric, tuning their understanding of it through peer and teacher feedback. During the assessment, they may refer to the rubric to think about how they can improve their responses. After the assessment, students can reflect on their own work and self-assess. If our ultimate goal is not just measurement but growth, this process of assessing with clear and consistent criteria, frequent feedback, and regular reflection is imperative.

Conclusion

Assessment often feels as if it has high stakes. Whether it's an end-of-the-year exam or a pop quiz in class, assessments can create anxiety for students, teachers, administrators, and parents. We know that some of our most difficult conversations and heated debates have been about assessment. While we agree that assessments are incredibly important and should be taken seriously by all stakeholders, it's imperative that we link assessments' importance and value to their purpose: understanding where students' are in their learning and how they can move forward as well as what is working about our instruction and where we need to improve.

As we pursue the goal of deepening students' understanding of conceptual relationships and their ability to transfer that understanding to grapple with novel contexts, we need to be intellectually honest with ourselves, our students, and all stakeholders about the data we are gathering from assessments. That kind of honesty is not always easy, but it's vital if we want to help our students grow. We also need to be rigorous about our assessment design to ensure that our assessments are focused on what we really want to measure. Now that you have the foundation, growing your practice will require lots of reflection, feedback from trusted colleagues, and experimentation. Mistakes are great ways to learn; that's as true for us as it is for our students! So keep the principles and examples of assessment for conceptual learning in mind, keep experimenting with personalized variations, keep pushing yourself and others to try new things, and keep reflecting on how it's all working. With that combination, we have no doubt your assessments will help your students on their journey for deep, conceptual understanding.

Chapter Review

- What is the purpose of assessment in conceptual teaching and learning?

- When during a unit should assessment take place? What types of assessment are appropriate at the beginning, middle, and end of a unit?

- How should students and teachers use the information gathered from assessments?

- What makes feedback effective?

- How can models, rubrics, student goal setting, and reflection help deepen students' conceptual understanding?

....

CHAPTER 6

How Can We Meet the Needs of All Learners in a Concept-Based Classroom?

T he concept of equity is enormous, and we struggled with whether it was too big to tackle as a chapter in this book. The National Equity Project's website defines equity this way: *"Educational equity means that each child receives what he or she needs to develop to his or her full academic and social potential"* ("Why Equity?," n.d.). Gender, social class, race, language, and learning difficulties are just some of the categories that affect equity. We decided to include this chapter because conceptual learning is an important piece of equity and we wanted to take it further with additional strategies. The ideas here will not come close to solving the enormous challenge of educational inequity, but the principles and strategies presented here should add to the conversation.

This chapter takes the reader through four key areas that are essential for equity:

1. Teacher **expectations** and **relationships** with students
2. Purposeful and **clear** goals, activities, instructions, and assessments
3. Constant collection of **evidence, feedback,** and **goal setting** by teacher and students
4. **Flexible grouping** based on what students **need at that moment** to reach the goal

First, it is still all too acceptable for teachers to use words like "weak students" or "smart students." This is a dangerous habit, as research shows us how easily these beliefs can be propagated and, fortunately, challenged (Dweck, 2007; Rosenthal & Jacobson, 2003). Students need to believe that their teacher is invested in their individual success (Hattie, 2012). Otherwise, instructional strategies aimed to serve the different needs of students are not likely to impact achievement. We have to *start* by challenging expectations and building relationships with students.

Second, recent research (Hattie, 2012; Marzano, 2007) supports what we have observed in countless classrooms and conversations with special educators. *Clarity* in classroom instructions and activities is an essential element for student achievement. Nearly every teacher falls victim to lack of clarity, often with the worthy goal of trying to make a learning experience "engaging." It is essential that every student understands the lesson goal and how each activity moves him or her closer to that goal.

Third, we need to be sure that assumptions are not influencing our decisions about how we group students or provide different learning experiences. Collecting *reliable data* becomes key. Preassessments tell us what students already know, understand, or misunderstand about a topic. Student goal setting, ongoing assessment, and timely, positive feedback let students know where they are in the learning journey.

Finally, once the first three prerequisites are in place, we can begin to differentiate instruction based on what students need at particular moments in the learning process. In equitable classrooms, we should see teachers who are both warm yet firm in their expectations, circulating among students who are all deeply invested in a clear and purposeful task that they know will help them advance in the learning journey. The following sections provide tools and tips for each of these four areas.

Shifting to a conceptual learning environment where students are guided to discover the relationships between concepts, supported by facts and specific contexts, is an important step in creating equitable classrooms. Most students—especially those who traditionally do poorly in school—thrive in an environment that centers on deep understanding and the application of learning in unique ways. When we ask students to find patterns and make connections, we give them intellectual dignity.

Therefore, Concept-Based Curriculum is naturally more equitable than a traditional, coverage-centered curriculum. When facts are *organized around key concepts,* it makes them *easier to remember.* This automatically benefits students who struggle with strict memorization without context or meaning. See 6.1 for an example.

FIGURE 6.1   VISUAL ARTS EXAMPLE

A student of visual arts learning about different artists and their corresponding works of art would be better able to memorize facts about the works if he or she discovered, through inquiry, that *converging lines can create the illusion of depth,* rather than simply trying to memorize aspects about a work without this depth of understanding.

Additionally, students are able to *find their own examples* that support their statements of conceptual relationship. This allows them to bring their own interests and experiences into their learning. Faster processors can be challenged to find more examples or even examples that complicate or contradict their relationship. See Figure 6.2 for an example.

FIGURE 6.2   POETRY EXAMPLE

Students studying poetry discover, through inquiry, that *word choice and rhythm shape the mood of a poem*. As a check for understanding, the teacher can ask students to select a poem of their choice on a topic of their choice and explain how the author's use of word choice and rhythm shaped the mood, using specific evidence from their chosen poem.

Furthermore, we can *gradually increase the complexity* of the statements of conceptual relationship in our lesson planning, starting with less complex statements and scaffolding to the goal of the unit. See Figure 6.3 for an example.

FIGURE 6.3   SCIENCE EXAMPLE

Concepts: equilibrium, environment, organisms

Statement of conceptual relationship: Most organisms must maintain an internal equilibrium in response to their environment.

Scaffolded statements:

1.   Organisms respond to their environment.
2.   Most organisms maintain an internal balance in order to survive.

Teachers exclaim time and time again how conceptual teaching and learning help students retain information and reach understanding on a deeper level. Figure 6.4 contains a reflection from a teacher we've worked with for several years. Her testimony reveals a unique strategy of starting with *examples of concepts in students' personal lives* and then linking them, through the concept, to the unit's content. Brilliant!

FIGURE 6.4   TEACHER TESTIMONY

Adopting conceptual teaching transformed my class at a high-poverty, urban school. Most of my students were highly skeptical of the government and were resistant to learning about civic principles they felt were "irrelevant" to their lives.

After learning about Concept-Based teaching, I opened each unit by identifying the sets of concepts at the foundation of government—individual rights vs. the common good; state rights vs. federal power; equality vs. freedom, etc.—and then helped them apply these sets of concepts to important issues in their neighborhoods and lives. The enthusiasm and engagement with which they approached the class that year contrasted markedly with student attitudes in previous years. And all but one of the 18-year-olds voted!

(Continued)

FIGURE 6.4   TEACHER TESTIMONY (CONTINUED)

Perhaps even more importantly, I found that conceptual teaching improved my success at reaching students with learning differences (IEPs). When I adopted conceptual teaching, I found that I could more effectively reach these students by starting the lesson with a very concrete example of the lesson's concept in their personal lives. Then I showed them how the personal example shared common attributes to the abstract concept. I then transferred this understanding to the unit's content or facts. This easy three-step process resulted in significantly deeper levels of understanding and engagement and transformed my students' ability to keep up with their peers. —Ayo Heinegg Magwood, Washington, DC

The Importance of Teacher Expectations and Relationships

Strategy #1: Take Action to Combat Low Expectations

There is an overwhelming amount of research that tells us how impactful adult expectations can be on student achievement (Marzano, 2007; Rosenthal & Jacobson, 2003). It's heart-wrenching and we almost wish we didn't have so much power over students—especially based on often-unconscious assumptions. Decades of research demonstrates that the interlocking factors of race, social class, and gender frequently lead to teachers making unconscious predictions about students (Eiland, 2008). We mispredict what students are capable of, and this can quickly become a self-fulfilling prophecy.

One of the earliest and most famous studies on this topic was conducted by Robert Rosenthal in 1964 (Rosenthal & Jacobson, 2003). Rosenthal gave elementary students from several different classes an IQ test. He randomly selected several students and told the teachers the test predicted that these particular students were going to experience a dramatic growth in IQ. Can you guess what happened? Following these students for two years, he found that these randomly selected kids did indeed have a growth in their IQ. How did this happen? Further research revealed that nearly imperceptible interactions from the teachers were the cause of this dramatic impact, from smiling at these students more to providing them with more specific feedback.

This research became known as the Pygmalion effect—where we subconsciously make predictions about students' abilities, often based on factors such as race and gender, and those predictions become reality. Later researchers such as Robert Pianta, dean of the Curry School of Education at the University of Virginia (Hamre & Pianta, 2006), and Robert Marzano (2007), showed that it is incredibly difficult for teachers to control their expectations of students. Both of these researchers agreed that *the key is to focus on teacher behaviors.*

The key is to focus on teacher behaviors.

We like Marzano's term "low-expectancy students," which is different from *low-skilled* students, as it focuses on the fact that some students are *expected* to be low achievers. It then becomes more motivating and effective to think, *"Let's take action to challenge the expectations of what this kid is capable of achieving and prove everyone wrong,"* rather than, *"He or she needs a lot more time and one-on-one attention to 'catch up.'"*

But teacher attitudes are only one part of the picture. Parent, peer, and students' own attitudes about their likelihood to succeed also contribute to students not reaching their full potential. As we challenge our assumptions, we need to consider what we can do to challenge other people's expectations of certain students as well.

Once you've identified a few of these low-expectancy students, it's time to take action. The steps listed in Figure 6.5 will make a huge difference on achievement (Hamre & Pianta, 2006; Marzano, 2007; Spiegel, 2012).

FIGURE 6.5 ACTION STEPS FOR TEACHER EXPECTATIONS

Action Step	Questions or Ideas to Consider
1. Make a list of students who typically perform below average and make notes at the end of the week about your interactions with them.	• Did I joke around with this student this week? Try to do this more often. • Did I use a harsh tone or become impatient with this student more than with other students? Try not to do this. • Did I check this student's work formally and informally (e.g., over the shoulder) and give him or her positive, constructive feedback?
2. Deliberately choose one or two small actions you will take with low-expectancy students over the course of a week.	• Seat them closer to you. • Make an effort to smile at them more. • Look them in the eye more. • Lean toward them more. • Be generally more friendly and supportive. • Call on them more often. • Ask them challenging questions. • Delve into their answers deeply. • Reward them only for rigorous responses.

(Continued)

FIGURE 6.5   ACTION STEPS FOR TEACHER EXPECTATIONS (CONTINUED)

3. Observe low-expectancy students, listen to their conversations with peers, and ask them questions about how they prefer to learn and their individual interests.	• What are his or her hobbies? • What motivates him or her? • How does he or she prefer to learn?
4. Try to react to challenging behaviors with calm and empathy. Students often misbehave to try and get attention. Count to three before reacting.	• Have I given this student positive attention lately? • How can I respond first with empathy? For example, *"I realize that it's hot in here today,"* or *"I understand that you want to answer the question and that is great; you just need to wait until I call on you."*
5. Try to spend time outside of your role as teacher, especially with low-expectancy students. Attend their basketball game, play games with them at recess, have a special breakfast or lunch with a small group, etc.	• What does this student do in his or her free time? • How can I engage in nonacademic activities with these students?
6. Find a way to learn about things they are interested in. Many students are skilled artists or athletes. Make note of how motivated or skilled they are in other areas of their lives.	• How does watching this student in a different context change my view of him or her?
7. Pay attention to signals that might tell you when certain students are having a bad day.	• What does this student's body language say today? • What might I say to this student if I notice he or she is having a bad day?
8. Structure class time to allow all students to have access to challenging materials and complex thought. Don't pull kids out frequently or divide classes into honors, etc.	• How have I challenged low-expectancy students this week? • Do I find myself pushing the thinking of certain students over others? • Does my grouping or the school's grouping subtly or overtly label students as high and low achievers?

Clarity of Goals, Instructions, Activities, and Assessments

Strategy #2: Work on Your Clarity

What do you notice about the classroom scenario described in Figure 6.6?

FIGURE 6.6   GEOMETRY EXAMPLE

> Unit goal: Length, width, and height determine the volume of different three-dimensional shapes.
>
> Grade 6 students are filling plastic geometric shapes with rice. They are working in groups of three, laughing and seeming to enjoy themselves and the activity. When asked "What is the purpose of this activity?" they respond with, "To see how much rice fits into each shape." When probed further about why that is important, they shrug and say, "I guess to see which shape is bigger by comparing how much rice each one holds."

Although this might seem like an exaggeration, we have observed hundreds of classrooms and asked hundreds of students the same question as in the scenario in Figure 6.6. And the vast majority of the time the answer is somewhat vague and not really connected to a rigorous learning goal. Although the activity is fun, hands-on, and likely has real academic value in the teacher's mind, the students are unsure about why they are doing it and how it is deepening their learning.

Here's an important clarification: We are huge fans of complex, messy, authentic, intellectual work. The trick is to make sure that the goal is clear and that the activity explicitly builds understanding toward the goal. And if the goal is a complex process—such as writing an argumentative essay—we try to focus on *one strategy or skill at a time*. We can layer on skills, knowledge, understanding, habits of mind, and so on. Many students get lost in a sea of messiness when the goal is unclear.

Even if the *task* is complex, the *instructions* need to be crystal clear. Simple directions lead to complex thinking, while complex directions often lead to fragmented, simple thinking. We need to show students what quality work looks like and what weak work looks like, discussing specifically what it is lacking. Rubrics, sample student work, and think-alouds are good tools to aid us in this endeavor.

> Even if the *task* is complex, the *instructions* need to be crystal clear.

Look at the classroom example in Figure 6.7 and identify the ways in which the teacher provides clarity to her students. Contrast this with the geometry example from Figure 6.6.

FIGURE 6.7 CLASSROOM EXAMPLE

The conceptual goal: *Novelists use vivid imagery to create a specific mood, often forcing the reader to empathize with the struggles of the central character.*

The teacher conducted a pretest at the start of the unit to see what students knew and understood about these literary concepts and their impact on the reader. Based on this information, she quickly reviewed some prerequisite knowledge that most of them had already mastered as well as retaught these skills to four students who seemed to need more in-depth review.

Before she conducted a discovery lesson on the conceptual understanding, she wanted to be sure they understood what a successful literary analysis looks like in general, so the next two lessons focused on that goal.

She posted a different conceptual understanding of literary devices she knew they all understood (she didn't share the exact understanding in order to allow students to discover it on their own) and conducted a think-aloud of a literary analysis to show students what goes on in her mind as she conducts one. Students used a rubric to evaluate her literary analysis example together as a class.

In groups, the students repeated the exercise using the rubric to evaluate a weak literary analysis (nonexample). She posted the instructions for the group work on the board, explained them aloud, and asked a student to state what they were supposed to do for the activity. Then she asked another student to explain how this activity would move them closer to mastering the goal of the unit, asked if everyone understood what they were supposed to do, clarified one student's question, and waited until 100% of students nodded their heads in agreement that they understood what to do before releasing them to do the group work.

The formative assessment gave students another literary analysis, and they had to *individually* repeat the same exercise they did in their group—evaluating the strengths and weaknesses of this new literary analysis. The teacher used the individual students' evaluation of the literary analysis to plan for the next two lessons, which explored the specific conceptual understanding, layering on this goal while also reteaching any students who needed more help on literary analysis.

What did you identify as efforts toward clarity in this teacher's classroom? Compare your findings with the steps outlined in Figure 6.8.

Every student should be able to answer the following questions during every lesson:

- What is the **goal**?
- What **exactly** should I be doing or thinking about in this moment?
- Why are we doing this activity and how does it **directly** relate to helping me reach the goal?

FIGURE 6.8   STEPS FOR CLARITY

1. Conduct a preassessment.
2. Review or reteach students who are lacking prerequisite knowledge.
3. Demonstrate what success looks like through model work and a think-aloud.
4. Utilize the rubric to evaluate strong and weak work.
5. Post instructions visually and explain aloud. Have a student explain in his or her own words, clarify any questions, and wait for 100% comprehension before moving on (*Note: If the teacher has earned the trust of students, most teens will be able to admit that they don't understand what to do—and strategies like this at least get those who are daydreaming to focus on the lesson*).
6. Use ongoing, formative assessments to allow students to practice.
7. Use data from the formative assessments to plan instruction.

Collecting and Analyzing Data

Strategy #3: Collect Ongoing Evidence So You and Your Students Know Exactly Where They Are in the Learning Journey; Give Feedback That Inspires Them to Work Harder

Once we have taken action toward students identified as low expectancy and spent time focused on becoming clearer on our goals, activities, and instructions, we are ready for the next step toward equitable classrooms. Chapter 5 contains specific tools for collecting ongoing, frequent evidence of individual student understanding through formative assessment. We then use this data to adjust instruction accordingly, such as reteaching certain students and providing extension activities to others.

We felt it worth repeating the importance of collecting ongoing evidence and providing feedback in this chapter on equity. In this context, we emphasize a most important point: We must disconnect historical or current data from possibility. For example, a secondary student reading at the third-grade level is still very capable of complex thinking. And English language learners are capable of more complex thought in their mother tongues than they can demonstrate in English. So while data is super important in the learning journey, we must take care to constantly build on strengths and identify ways to draw out students' full potential. We must use more than one data point when making decisions and try to use a mixture of quantitative data and qualitative data.

> We must disconnect historical or current data from possibility.

When we assess, we have to be careful not to crowd an assessment item with a lot of noise that is not targeting precisely what we want to measure. For example, if recall of specific information is not important to you, add a word bank. If you don't need students to remember specific steps when asking for application, list the steps on the assessment. We also need to provide accommodations for students with specific learning difficulties. For instance, if there is a lot of text on an exam, it can be read aloud to a student with dyslexia.

For the purpose of equity, the importance of providing *specific, positive feedback* on students' progress toward the learning goal cannot be overstated. Teachers must consider the point of view of the students and think about what information will be most useful in motivating them and moving them along in the learning process. Ask yourself, "If I were this student, what would I want to hear to help motivate me to work hard to reach the goal?" and "How can I make this feedback positive?"

For example, if a student typically has trouble writing a paragraph, and the task was to write an essay, instead of saying "you are far away from writing an essay," communicate the increase in growth on writing a single paragraph, if that is evident in the work sample. Constantly emphasizing what the student has not yet mastered is called the deficit model—and it doesn't work in helping kids accelerate quickly. It is more effective to build on students' strengths.

Research on minority students attending predominately White colleges showed an incredibly powerful formula for feedback that motivates students. First, repeat the standard of excellence we are aiming to achieve. Second, point to pieces of their work that demonstrate they are capable of reaching the standard. Third, make recommendations for what to improve on next to move closer to the standard (Steele, 2011).

Implementing and Managing a Differentiated Classroom

Once we've actively worked on addressing our **attitudes** about students and our **clarity** in all classroom activities and collecting **evidence** of student understanding, then, and only then, are we ready for students to be working on different things at the same time in class. In addition to students working on different activities, we should also remember to vary the means of whole group instruction such as using visual, audio, hands-on, or calisthenic activities to increase the chances of students grasping the intended goals.

Differentiated instruction varies among different configurations such as:

- Individual work time on different tasks
- Heterogeneous groups of students teaching or providing feedback to each other
- Teacher conferencing or reteaching certain students

Differentiation is about giving students *exactly* what they need at *particular moments* in the learning journey based on *ongoing evidence* collected from formative assessments. This can include extension activities beyond the target learning goal for students who are ready for more complex work.

Individuals or groups of students can be:

- Reading a complex text or primary source
- Giving feedback on one another's work
- Doing practice exercises
- Taking a quiz
- Watching a video
- Listening to a podcast
- Playing an online game
- Using flash cards to build memory of key terms or ideas
- Receiving more or less scaffolding such as sentence stems, examples, and nonexamples

Strategy #4: Consider These Steps to Differentiate in a Concept-Based Classroom

Step 1. Assessment: After conducting a preassessment you will know what different students need at the start of the unit. Figure 6.9 provides some ideas for responding to typical points of confusion.

A few typical outcomes from preassessment data:

- Some will need more clarification of the *concepts themselves* while others will already have a solid grasp. For example, in science class, some students may think equilibrium means equal rather than a balance. In social studies, some students may think of power only as formal political power and will need to expand their view.
- It is also common that some students have a *misunderstanding* of the conceptual relationship, which needs to be corrected.
- Finally, it is very typical for some students to have an *overly simplistic* understanding of the conceptual relationship. This is where you would scaffold the complexity of the statement and look for contexts that illustrate the increasing complexity.

Step 2. Planning: When first starting differentiation, we recommend placing students in two or three groups. That will feel more manageable—but be sure that you do not reinforce low-expectancy grouping. As you become more skilled at planning for differentiation, you can plan more than three different activities. Example: One group does the concept attainment activity explained in Chapter 3, while another group begins experimenting with conceptual relationships. Consider using learning stations and giving students options.

FIGURE 6.9   RESPONDING TO ASSESSMENT DATA

Assessment result	Possible Instructional Strategies	Example
Weak understanding of the concept(s)	• Conduct a concept attainment activity. • Use flash cards (Quizlet). • Match scenarios to concepts.	Math students sort cards into examples and nonexamples of *functions*.
Misunderstanding of the conceptual relationship	• Match relationship to examples. • Make a visual map of understanding. • Test hypothesis to disprove misconception.	Music students match statements about the relationship between *harmony* and *tone* to pieces of music.
Overly simplistic understanding of the conceptual relationship	• Match examples with two concepts then tell the relationship. • Ask "why," "how," or "so what." • Work down the Structure of Knowledge or Structure of Process. • Students provide peer feedback.	Social studies students read examples of the relationship between *war* and *leadership* and try to determine and articulate the relationship.
Solid understanding of the conceptual relationship	• Introduce complications. • Make own Structure of Knowledge diagram or Structure of Process diagram. • Transfer to new situations. • Peer teach. • Provide feedback to peers.	Science students transfer understanding of the relationship between *homeostasis* and *adaptation* to a new, complex situation.

Step 3. Execution: Unfortunately, most secondary students are conditioned to do almost nothing without constant direction from a teacher. They usually will not immediately work well in more self-directed learning environments. Consider the tips listed in Figure 6.10 to establish effective use of precious class time.

FIGURE 6.10   TIPS FOR EFFECTIVE DIFFERENTIATION

Tips:	Might look like:
Teach students how to work effectively in groups.	• Students take three minutes to jot down what makes teamwork successful and discuss with their group. • Students evaluate each other on participation. • Teachers evaluate students on participation. • Provide sentence stems to help solicit participation from reluctant or quiet students. "_____, what do you think?" • Use protocols to guide equitable collaboration. • Use group roles to help structure teamwork.
Teach students how to work independently and to keep going even when they feel stuck. (*We've witnessed way too much wasted class time while students sit and wait for the teacher to finish conferencing with another group.*)	• Classroom rule: You cannot stop work while waiting for the teacher; move on to something else or just try to move forward before getting help. • Create a norm where students have to ask three students for help before asking the teacher. • Give hypothetical scenarios and discuss how students can move on even while waiting for the teacher. • Use some sort of simple signal like putting a card with a question mark face-up on the desk so the teacher knows the student needs help.
Utilize the rubric and student goal setting so they know why they are working on what they are working on at that moment.	• Students glue the rubric to the inside cover of their notebook and refer to it every day for reflection. • Students identify one area where they've improved to celebrate success.

(Continued)

FIGURE 6.10   TIPS FOR EFFECTIVE DIFFERENTIATION (CONTINUED)

Tips:	Might look like:
Mix teacher-directed activities with student choice.	• Some days explain the different learning activities or stations and let students choose what makes the most sense given where they are in the learning journey.
Conference with students regularly.	• Listen to students, try to figure out from them how you can help them learn better.
Reteach or provide minilessons when students need it.	• When a majority of the students are misunderstanding a key point, pull attention to the front of the room to reexplain to everyone at the same time rather than going group to group to reexplain the same thing. • During small group or one-on-one sessions, ask a lot of questions, allow students to admit areas of confusion, and construct meaning for themselves in this more private space.
Collect and save your materials.	• Laminate images or other materials to be used over and over again. • Different groups can use the same materials on different days. • It is likely that the concepts and examples will resurface throughout the school year.
Be sure to vary the groups! If you find yourself keeping students in the same groups (particularly if they can be viewed as "slower" and "faster" groups) for more than a few lessons, then it's time to work harder on taking action toward low-expectancy students.	• Talk with students who still seem to be struggling after a few days to brainstorm together ways to support them. • Include independent work regularly, even for just a few minutes. • Play games with mixed groups. • Use different activities that allow different students to shine (e.g., drawing, calisthenic activity outside).

Tips for Inclusive Classrooms

It is common practice to pair a special educator with a subject-specific teacher in many secondary classrooms, but we have found that few schools provide structures or training for effective use of this arrangement. It can often feel like the subject teacher is "in charge" and the special educator is more like an aid than an equal partner. We've also seen many teachers view the special educator as the one to solve the "problems" with students who learn differently. This should not be the case.

The goal of the relationship between a general educator and a special educator is to build the general educator's own capacity in reaching all students. The special educator should be working to coach the general educator on strategies and when to employ them. Their collaboration could alternate between coplanning, offering feedback, and modeling lesson plans for students. After a few coplanning sessions, the general education teacher should have collected enough strategies to be able to plan for accommodations on his or her own, without the special educator present.

To facilitate coplanning based on the principles in this chapter, we've created a potential list of questions in Figure 6.11 to use during coplanning sessions.

FIGURE 6.11 QUESTIONS TO FACILITATE COPLANNING FOR INCLUSIVE CLASSROOMS

- What is the learning goal for the day? If it is a complex process, which strategy or skill are we focused on for this lesson?
- How will students know what quality work looks like?
- How does each learning activity move students toward that goal?
- How will we ensure the instructions for each activity are clear and understood?
- How will we collect evidence on whether individual students are on track toward achieving the goal?
- How well do our formative and summative assessments measure precisely what it is we want to measure?
- How will we give positive and specific feedback to students all along the learning journey process?
- How will we provide support for those who need extra help?
- How will we show increased attention to low-expectancy students (e.g., smile more, use their names more, give more feedback, get to them know personally)?

Teacher Self-Assessment for Equitable Classrooms

A deep commitment to equity is an important goal, especially in today's diverse classrooms. We frequently use the self-assessment in Figure 6.12 to reflect on our own practice and try to identify ways to improve. Try it out and see where you might want to focus your efforts.

FIGURE 6.12   TEACHER SELF-ASSESSMENT ON EQUITABLE CLASSROOMS

Teacher Self-Assessment on Equitable Classrooms				
How well do I employ the following teaching strategies?	Never ←		→	Daily
Attitudes and Expectations of Students				
I choose low-expectancy students and focus on giving more attention, smiles, feedback, and praise.	1	2	3	4
Clarity of Goals, Activities, and Instructions				
Students have a clear picture of what quality work looks like and what they need to do to achieve the goal.	1	2	3	4
My learning activities always clearly and completely move students toward the learning target.	1	2	3	4
My instructions for each activity are simple and clear.	1	2	3	4
Evidence Collection and Feedback for Students				
My assessments clearly measure the precise learning target and do not contain any unnecessary "noise."	1	2	3	4
I collect individual evidence of student understanding.	1	2	3	4
I give individual, positive, and effective feedback to students about where they are in the learning journey.	1	2	3	4
Differentiated Activities				
I modify instruction based on data collected showing where students are in the learning journey.	1	2	3	4
Students work in flexible groups, individually or with me based on what they need at that moment. I do not use fixed, homogenous groups.	1	2	3	4

Conclusion

This chapter provides a few principles and strategies to move toward creating a more equitable learning environment for all students. We must constantly remind ourselves of the enormous power we have as teachers. We need to get in the habit of consistently checking our expectations of students and working toward building solid relationships with each of them, especially those who do not typically do well in school. Through positive interactions, clear instructions, and solid use of data to inform flexible grouping, we can help each student reach his or her potential.

Chapter Review

- What is the relationship between teacher expectations and equity? What might you say to a peer the next time you hear something like "my weak student"?
- How does clarity of goals, activities, instructions, and assessments foster equity?
- What role does evidence collecting, feedback, and goal setting have in equitable classrooms?
- Why are flexible groups essential for equitable classrooms? What does fixed grouping communicate to students?

....

CHAPTER 7

What Is the Relationship Between Current Best Practices and Concept-Based Curriculum and Instruction?

Teaching is incredibly complex. This chapter is an effort to help teachers make connections between some of the current education improvement initiatives and Concept-Based Curriculum and Instruction. We've tried to integrate many best practices into our tools, descriptions, and frameworks. Hopefully you've noticed this alignment before this chapter!

Just as having a conceptual framework helps students learn, recall, and use information and skills, our hope is that using Concept-Based teaching and learning as a lens will help these initiatives seem less like disparate facts and more like an organized system of knowledge that you can use flexibly. To that end, we find it helpful to categorize educational initiatives and research as being curricular, instructional, or assessment oriented. See Figure 7.1 for an idea of how we categorize the best practices outlined in this chapter. Although it may not be obvious, when you dig into many initiatives you'll see that they are complementary and can be integrated to form a coherent learning experience for students.

In this chapter we'll discuss several popular educational initiatives and their connection to conceptual teaching and learning. Seeing these connections will both help you create an integrated understanding of these initiatives and share that understanding with colleagues. Our hope is that rather than seeing conceptual teaching as "one more thing to do," this chapter will provide you with a compass for navigating approaches and interpreting the sometimes muddy waters of education initiatives.

FIGURE 7.1   EDUCATION INITIATIVES BY CATEGORY

Curricular Goals	Instruction	Assessment
• Understanding by Design • International Baccalaureate • Common Core State Standards (CCSS), Next Generation Science Standards (NGSS), C3 Social Studies Standards • Advanced Placement (AP)	• Cooperative Learning • Technology	• SAT • Every Student Succeeds Act (ESSA)

Concepts and Understanding by Design (UbD)

The work of Wiggins and McTighe (2005), with its emphasis on enduring understandings that move beyond surface level and are supported by corresponding facts and skills, is perhaps the curriculum framework most similar to Concept-Based Curriculum and Instruction. Both models are idea-centered curriculum design efforts. Both use questions as the primary means of conveying curriculum goals and as the first means of engaging the minds of students.

The main difference between the models is centered on Erickson and Lanning's (2014) explanations of the Structure of Knowledge and Process. These authors more clearly and succinctly demonstrate the relationship between concepts, facts, and skills. Using these structures, conceptual learning requires us to articulate the enduring understandings as relationships between two or more concepts. This can sometimes feel more prescriptive than Wiggins and McTighe's (2005) *Understanding by Design* (UbD) guidelines for crafting enduring understandings, which do not specify the role of concepts.

UbD divides enduring understandings into two categories: overarching and topical. Topical understandings do not align to the Concept-Based model, since they are not designed to transfer beyond the topic of study. For instance, a topical understanding might be, "The Watergate crisis weakened public trust in government."

Overarching understandings, on the other hand, are meant to convey larger transferable insights. Wiggins and McTighe (2005) provided the following as an example: "Democracy requires a free and courageous press, willing to question authority" (p. 131). Notice that this generalization puts concepts into relationship with one another. The authors wrote, "the specific topics, events, or texts of the unit are typically not mentioned in the overarching understanding" (p. 114). While Wiggins and McTighe's overarching understandings and Erickson and Lanning's generalizations are very similar, the Concept-Based work of Erickson and Lanning offers greater insight into the process of creating these types of generalizations and exactly how to design curriculum that will help students arrive at them.

The two efforts can easily coexist. You can use the UbD unit planner, "6 Facets of Understanding" rubric, GRASPS performance assessment model, and WHERETO instructional planning acronym alongside your Concept-Based Curriculum design. There are a few important points to remember:

- Write statements of conceptual relationship as your enduring understandings.
- Ensure that there are adequate corresponding questions, facts, and skills that connect to each big idea.
- Align learning experiences to the concepts.
- Provide instructional contexts that help to reveal the relationship among the concepts.
- Be sure to design performance assessments that measure students' understanding of the conceptual relationships.

Concepts and Cooperative Learning

Many schools are embracing the power of cooperative learning, which involves students learning from one another through group tasks that emphasize collaboration and team effort. Cooperative learning techniques include simple strategies like think-pair-share and jigsaws as well as long-term group projects. These techniques can be contrasted with teacher-centered approaches to learning. Direct instruction strategies such as lectures or presentations, where students primarily take and process information individually, are not cooperative in nature. Because conceptual teaching and learning rely on student inquiry and uncoverage, rather than an overreliance on direct instruction, they naturally lend themselves to cooperative learning.

A few cooperative learning strategies that are particularly useful in the Concept-Based classroom include the following:

1. **Heterogeneous groupings:** Students benefit from working in groups of mixed abilities, passions, and perspectives. Place students in heterogeneous groups when you want them to challenge and complicate each other's thinking about the concepts. Placing students in groups where they are apt to disagree with each other will require them to focus on the evidence that supports their generalizations and to face evidence that doesn't fit. Also, having them in mixed-readiness groups can help students provide support for one another.

2. **Homogenous groupings:** It can also be helpful to include students with similar working styles, skill levels, and points of view. This allows you to

differentiate texts, lines of questioning, pace of work, student products, and other elements of the inquiry process to ensure all students have opportunities to think about the concepts for themselves. Be sure to avoid placing students too frequently in homogenous groups or associating any status with the different groups. If you are not careful, homogenous groups can lead to students labeling themselves and one another in ways that can interfere with their sense of belonging and growth mindset.

3. **Barn-raising activities:** A "barn-raising" strategy is one in which all members of a group or class work together to "build" an idea, much like a community might come together to build a barn. Small groups begin with a statement of conceptual relationship developed by one student and "build it up" together as teams. They think of as many supporting examples and pieces of evidence as they can. Then they work to refine the statement together, making it more clear, precise, or accurate.

4. **Inquiry stations:** This strategy requires student groups to rotate through several case studies, using each to develop and refine their understanding of conceptual relationships. At each station, groups should watch a video, read a text, ponder a problem, or complete a task designed to inform their understanding of the concepts.

Conceptual learning goals are nearly always compatible with cooperative learning strategies, but students also need time to think about concepts individually. We like to think about striking at least a 75:25 balance. When using a cooperative learning model, about three quarters of class time should be devoted to student collaboration; students learn best through interactions with others, and this type of learning—debating, discussing, problem solving, peer questioning—takes time. However, at least one quarter of instructional time should be reserved for individual idea development and reflection. For instance, a 60-minute class period might involve 40 to 45 minutes of small group discussion, with 5 to 10 minutes of individual journaling at the end, along with a few minutes of teacher-directed framing and closure. Thinking about a longer period of time, a good balance might be three days engaging in lab experiments with partners, with a fourth day reserved for drawing individual conclusions and creating a personal concept map.

The products of individual work, such as journal entries, lab reports, transfer tasks, and problem sets, help us collect data on each student's understanding of the concepts and ability to apply the concepts in unfamiliar situations.

Concepts and Technology

Many schools have made it a priority to expose students to 21st-century technologies by introducing iPads and laptops into classrooms, carving out "makerspaces," and investing in expensive equipment like laser cutters, 3-D printers, and drones. Some schools have adopted new policies, like "bring your own device" (BYOD), to adjust to the increasingly important role that technology plays in kids' lives. This has left teachers in the difficult position of figuring out how to deal with technology both as a teaching tool and as a distraction, often resulting in a frustrating experience.

Conceptual teaching and learning can help.

Using technology to access information: The greatest advantage of the Internet is that it provides students with instant access to a wide variety of information. For conceptual teaching and learning, that means that many different contexts are easily available to help students develop, test, and transfer their conceptual understanding. Consider harnessing (rather than fighting) the power of the web in the following ways:

1. Design conceptual inquiry webquests. A webquest is an inquiry task where the majority of learning inputs come from the Internet. Pose a conceptual question and set a product goal for students. For instance, you might tell students their quest is to investigate the relationship among symmetry, shape, and measurement in order to design a stained glass window that employs these concepts. Then point students toward articles, videos, simulations, or other web-based resources to help them understand the concepts and achieve their goal.

2. Incorporate research on concepts. Ask students to find their own contexts or situations in which the concepts being studied play a key role. Students can then share the scenarios they have found and evaluate which are the strongest match with the concepts.

3. Expose students to a wider variety of perspectives. Move beyond the textbook or teacher as the source of information about the concepts. Seek out controversial points of view and contradictory opinions on the Internet and assign students to explore and discuss ways of thinking about the concepts. Also, challenge students to find evidence that contradicts their generalizations. Then discuss the process they used to find this information and how they assessed the reliability of the information they found.

Using technology to connect and collaborate: Access to the Internet has also expanded the boundaries of the classroom. Consider the following opportunities to deepen conceptual understanding and transfer through technology-enabled collaboration:

1. Connect students to experts in the field through video chats, email correspondence, or live chat features. How powerful would it be for physics students studying the relationship between compressional and tensional stress to interview engineers who design and maintain bridges? Have students develop questions that will inform their conceptual understanding ahead of time to maximize this interaction.

2. Provide real-world audiences for students' work products. Assemble a virtual "panel" to judge students' essays, artwork, documentaries, designs, and proposals. For instance, students studying the relationship among line, color, proportion, and dimension in visual art might design their own art pieces and solicit feedback from artists near and far through a series of personal video conferences or by publishing their work on a class website.

3. Encourage collaboration outside of class. Ask students to provide feedback on each other's statements of conceptual relationship using Google Docs or create a group mind map that shows the relationship among concepts and facts using Coggle. Ask students to contribute to a group discussion forum about the concepts a few times per week by sharing new ideas and responding directly to their peers at their own pace.

Using technology to create and innovate: New technologies also enable students to create products that put their conceptual understanding to use. For instance, 10th-grade geometry students studying the relationship among the concepts of volume, surface area, scale, and similarity might use a 3-D printer to create visual aids to help them explain these concepts to a third-grade class. English language arts students studying the relationship among audience, purpose, and word choice may show their understanding by designing a social media campaign to support a cause that is important to them, tailoring the word choice to a variety of potential audiences.

A good way to ensure that the technology doesn't overwhelm the conceptual learning goals is to require students to compose a written reflection about how their understanding of the concepts influenced their final product.

Concepts and Common Core State Standards, NGSS, C3 Framework

In the past few years there have been several new standards frameworks released in the United States, namely, the Common Core State Standards (CCSS), the Next Generation Science Standards (NGSS), and the C3 Social Studies Standards. These new standards seek to provide guidance for teachers, school leaders, and policy makers in preparing students for college, career, and civic life in the 21st century. Though these frameworks span the disciplines, building conceptual understanding is a key focus and priority for each. Not only does conceptual teaching and learning support the ultimate goals of these standards, they are also explicitly named as essential elements in each.

The CCSS are the most well known and most controversial of these frameworks. They tackle primarily math and English language arts (reading, writing, speaking, and listening) standards, with additional standards for literacy in science and social studies. We won't discuss the political debates regarding the CCSS and the testing that is often linked with discussions of the standards. Instead, we'll focus on the content of the standards themselves, which, in absence of the policy ramifications, we would argue are helpful guidelines for designing learning experiences for students.

The major goal of the CCSS is to backward-map a trajectory of skills and knowledge that would prepare students for success in higher education and careers, as well as the more difficult to quantify yet incredibly important area of preparing students for civic engagement. To that end, the authors of the CCSS sought to create "fewer and higher" benchmarks for student learning. Their goal was to design a set of standards that would be essential, rigorous, clear, specific, coherent, and internationally benchmarked. To achieve that goal, the authors explained that a few criteria drove their design of the standards. In the authors' own language, those criteria included the following:

- "Rigorous: The standards will include high-level cognitive demands by asking students to demonstrate **deep conceptual understanding** through **the application of content knowledge and skills to new situations** [emphasis added].
- Coherent: The standards should convey a **unified vision of the big ideas and supporting concepts** [emphasis added] within a discipline and reflect a progression of learning that is meaningful and appropriate" (National Governors, 2010).

The authors of the CCSS synthesized great amounts of educational research along with the experience of teachers and leaders across the country to develop these criteria and the standards that followed. Building conceptual understanding is highlighted as an important aim of the standards. Undeniably, a conceptual approach to teaching and learning is aligned with the overall goals of the CCSS. See Figure 7.2 for direct quotes from the standards or from speeches by developers of the standards that support conceptual learning.

Like the CCSS, the NGSS explicitly seek to develop students' progressive understanding of disciplinary concepts. The introduction to these standards reads:

> Every NGSS standard has three dimensions: disciplinary core ideas (content), scientific and engineering practices, and cross-cutting concepts. . . . The NGSS encourage integration with multiple core concepts throughout each year. Science concepts build coherently across K–12. The emphasis of the NGSS is a focused and coherent progression of knowledge from grade band to grade band, allowing for a dynamic process of building knowledge throughout a student's entire K–12 scientific education. (NGSS Lead States, 2013)

FIGURE 7.2 CONCEPTS IN THE COMMON CORE STATE STANDARDS

CCSS Math	CCSS English Language Arts
"The Common Core concentrates on a clear set of math skills and concepts. Students will learn concepts in a more organized way both during the school year and across grades. The standards encourage students to solve real-world problems" (National Governors, 2010). – CCSS Mathematical Standards Introduction	"The core standards thus mark a shift. They do support training in narrative throughout K-12, but what they make primary as you grow is the ability to write an argument based on evidence and convey complex information. This is an essential shift." (Coleman, 2011). —Speech by David Coleman, lead developer of the CCSS and president and chief executive officer of the College Board
For example: In CCSS-aligned mathematics classrooms, students must balance conceptual understanding with procedural fluency. For example, a sixth-grade standard asks students to: *Understand the concept of a ratio and use ratio language to describe a ratio relationship between two quantities.* (CCSS.MATH.CONTENT.7.RP.A.1) Another sixth-grade standard requires students to be able to: *Use ratio reasoning to convert measurement units; manipulate and transform units appropriately when multiplying or dividing quantities.* (CCSS.MATH.CONTENT.7.RP.A.3.D) For the first standard, students must understand the concept of a ratio, a task that likely requires them to explore multiple examples, deepening their understanding of this important mathematical idea as they go. The second standard, though related to the first, asks students to complete the more procedural task for converting measurement	**For example:** One of the foundational standards in the CCSS for writing is defending claims with evidence. This standard spirals throughout the grade levels and in sixth grade it states that students should be able to: *Write arguments to support claims with clear reasons and relevant evidence.* (CCSS.ELA-LITERACY.W.7.1) At first glance the connection between this standard and conceptual teaching and learning might not be clear. Yet, there are two ways this standard suggests a conceptual approach to teaching and learning. The first is in the structure of CCSS for English language arts. As mentioned earlier, this standard spirals throughout the framework, calling for increasing sophistication in students' ability to defend their claims. In this context, we see a clear connection between the CCSS and the Structure of Process. Students need to explore the disciplinary concepts of claims, reasons, and evidence and their relationship to one another. Their understanding of this relationship should increase with sophistication over time.

	In addition, the CCSS does not specify particular content that English language arts teachers need to cover (with the exception of Shakespeare and founding documents). Instead English language arts teachers are free to structure their content
units. While our hope is that students will complete this process with the foundation of understanding the concept of ratios, they need to show they have mastered the process of converting units with fluency. We don't want students to have to think through the concept of ratio each time they need to convert measurement units—that should be almost automatic after practice—but we do want them to have the tools to figure out novel problems that might be outside of the realm of their automaticity by applying their conceptual understanding.	in a way that best supports students' development as critical readers/ listeners and powerful writers/ speakers. Learning those skills through a conceptual approach helps students dig deeper into their reading and grow as writers. This includes both disciplinary concepts like those discussed earlier and universal concepts, such as those explored by many authors in both literacy and informational texts. To build their conceptual understanding, students should engage in exactly the reading, writing, speaking, and listening practices that standards promote: reading closely, using evidence from the text to build understanding, and defending claims with evidence. Thus the CCSS builds students' discipline-specific conceptual frameworks and also allows flexibility for teachers and school leaders to design the content of English language arts units around powerful concepts that will enrich students' development as critical thinkers, readers, and writers.

Furthermore, the authors of NGSS argue:

> To develop a thorough understanding of scientific explanations of the world, students need sustained opportunities to work with and develop the underlying ideas and to appreciate those ideas' interconnections over a period of years rather than weeks or months. (NGSS Lead States, 2013)

The NGSS are undoubtedly designed to foster conceptual learning. In fact, one of the more damaging missteps that educators could make when implementing these standards would be to teach them as if they were unconnected facts rather than an interconnected conceptual framework. The structure of the NGSS is actively working to combat that possibility and promote students developing the real-world thinking that scientists use to grapple with, explore, and understand our world.

The social studies counterpart to the NGSS and the CCSS is the National Council for the Social Studies' College, Career, and Civic Life (C3) Framework for Social Studies State Standards. Similar to the other standards frameworks we have discussed, the introduction to the C3 standards outlines the importance of a conceptual approach to social studies:

> The C3 Framework is centered on an Inquiry Arc—a set of interlocking and mutually supportive ideas that frame the ways students learn social studies content. By focusing on inquiry, the framework emphasizes the disciplinary concepts and practices that support students as they develop the capacity to know, analyze, explain, and argue about interdisciplinary challenges in our social world. ("The College," 2013)

Furthermore, the authors of the framework suggest their purpose is to help students develop

> the intellectual power to recognize societal problems; ask good questions and develop robust investigations into them; consider possible solutions and consequences; separate evidence-based claims from parochial opinions; and communicate and act upon what they learn. And most importantly, they must possess the capability and commitment to repeat that process as long as is necessary. Young people need strong tools for, and methods of, clear and disciplined thinking in order to traverse successfully the worlds of college, career, and civic life. ("The College," 2013)

As we have discussed throughout this book, teaching students to think conceptually allows them to conduct the type of "robust investigations" that the authors of C3 intend. Developing a conceptual framework allows students to carry out in-depth inquiry that strengthens their conceptual understanding, helps them to retain factual information, and allows them to unlock novel situations. Conceptual understanding is an essential tool in helping students understand and act in the world around them.

The CCSS, the NGSS, and the C3 framework represent the foremost expert thinking on standards for each of the traditional core four disciplines: math, social studies, science, and English language arts. The standards in each of these frameworks explicitly seek to build students' conceptual understanding in service of preparing them for college, career, and civic life. If you are working with these standards, conceptual teaching and learning are not layers you have to add to your practice. They comprise a cohesive lens to help you approach your work across the disciplines.

Concepts and the International Baccalaureate (IB)

The Concept-Based work of Erickson and Lanning is very popular among International Baccalaureate (IB) schools around the globe. The IB curriculum is explicit and deliberate about building conceptual understanding from the primary years through the final two years of secondary school. In 2012, Erickson published a position paper through the IB organization. She commended their curriculum design efforts, and her praise is well-deserved. She also offered a few suggestions or changes that we also endorse. Following are some key points from her paper:

1. More **disciplinary-depth,** especially in the Primary Years Programme (PYP) and the Middle Years Programme (MYP)—What Erickson calls micro-concepts, the IB calls related concepts, as in "related" to a subject-specific discipline rather than transdisciplinary. The examples offered in the MYP guide, *Principles to Practice,* are a good first step, but there are many more specific concepts per discipline that should be included in the three to five years of the MYP. For example, in mathematics, the related concepts include pattern and measurement, but they should also include more microconcepts such as slope, angle, and function. This move will better prepare students for the disciplinary rigor of the Diploma Programme (DP).

2. **More than one statement** of conceptual relationship per unit—The Central Idea (PYP), Statement of Inquiry (MYP), and the Essential Idea (DP) are the equivalent to Erickson's use of the words *generalization* or *principle.* A good rule of thumb is five to nine statements per unit, depending on the length of the unit and age level of the students. The units are often several weeks long, and one statement of conceptual relationship is simply not enough to build disciplinary depth and understanding.

Our work with IB schools reinforces these areas of need:

1. More emphasis on **conceptual relationships**—Our work with IB schools demonstrates a strong commitment to concepts, but it's the conceptual relationships that allow students to unlock new situations. Simply understanding the concepts themselves in isolation is not enough. This is often an "aha moment" for IB teachers attending our workshops.

2. More emphasis on **synergistic thinking,** the relationship between conceptual understanding and factual information—Some IB schools shift the pendulum too far in the direction of transferable concepts without grounding them enough in key facts and skills. The importance of facts in supporting conceptual understanding is also often a new insight for IB teachers who attend our workshops.

3. More questions to drive inquiry—Students should **uncover the relationship** between the concepts through inquiry. Posting the statement on the wall tends to invoke less interest among students. Instead, post the questions that help students to uncover the conceptual relationships.

4. More emphasis on the importance of **disciplinary transfer**—The goal is for students to transfer their learning within the discipline as well as across disciplines. We have found that teachers, especially at the PYP and the MYP level, are singularly focused on helping students transfer their learning to other subject areas. While this is a key feature of conceptual learning, teachers also need to realize and appreciate the value of disciplinary transfer.

Concepts and Advanced Placement (AP) and SAT

The College Board has also recognized the importance of conceptual learning, and this has been reflected in their redesigned Advanced Placement (AP) courses and SAT tests. While previous versions of AP and SAT tests left students and teachers with the impression that mounds of facts, isolated skills, and arbitrary vocabulary words were most important, the new AP and SAT frameworks better reflect the skills and knowledge that make students college ready. These changes align well with Concept-Based Curriculum and Instruction. Consider two major changes to the SAT reading test:

- Words in context: Rather than testing vocabulary recall, the new SAT asks students to figure out the meaning of words presented in authentic contexts.

- Command of evidence: Reading questions ask students to select the best evidence from a passage to support a point or evaluate an author's use of evidence.

And consider changes to the SAT math section, which now focuses on three major competencies:

- Fluency: Students must show that they can identify an efficient strategy for solving a problem and carry it out with flexibility and accuracy.

- Conceptual understanding: Making connections between math concepts, operations, and relations is now a major focus of the test.

- Application: According to the College Board (2016b), "These real-world problems ask [students] to analyze a situation, determine the essential elements required to solve the problem, represent the problem mathematically, and carry out a solution."

The connections between these focus areas and a Concept-Based classroom are clear. In math there is an explicit recognition of the power and importance of students building a conceptual framework and applying their understanding of concepts to complex real-world problems. Conceptual teaching will also prepare students for the revised reading SAT. Conceptual learning prioritizes students taking command of their **own thinking** by discovering conceptual relationships for themselves. It is characterized by extended periods of **text-based inquiry** with the goal of uncovering profound truths about the world students live in. It requires students to defend their generalizations with a **wide array of evidence** and examples. It values **authentic transfer of learning** to new, unfamiliar, real-world situations. All this hones students' ability to figure out a new understanding based on evidence. This type of thinking is exactly what students need to succeed on the new SAT.

The new AP course designs also reflect the importance of conceptual relationships and encourage conceptual teaching. Each course is based on a "concept outline," which states the big ideas at the heart of the course. Embedded in these big ideas are some of the most powerful conceptual relationships for each discipline. The College Board curriculum committees for each course—high school teachers, college professors, and other disciplinarians—have developed a few big ideas and then listed supporting topical understandings and factual knowledge. To the discerning eye, the Structure of Knowledge is easily visible in the AP concept outlines! Consider the following big ideas or enduring understandings from the outlines of redesigned AP courses:

- AP Chemistry: Chemical and physical properties of materials can be explained by the structure and the arrangement of atoms, ions, or molecules and the forces between them. (College Board, 2014)

- AP Biology: Biological systems utilize free energy and molecular building blocks to grow, to reproduce, and to maintain dynamic homeostasis. (College Board, 2015a)

- AP Calculus AB: Continuity is a key property of functions that is defined using limits. (College Board, 2016a)

- AP European History: Cities offered economic opportunities, which attracted increasing migration from rural areas, transforming urban life and creating challenges for the new urbanites and their families. (College Board, 2015b)

- AP United States History: Different native societies adapted to and transformed their environments through innovations in agriculture, resource use, and social structure. (College Board, 2015c)

These redesigned courses reflect the growing body of research about what type of learning serves students best. The College Board (2012) cited studies by the National Research Council, among others, as the basis for rethinking its courses to place greater emphasis on inquiry, critical thinking, reasoning, communication, and balancing breadth of knowledge with depth of understanding. There is also a significant emphasis on disciplinary ways of thinking and doing, an approach that mirrors the Structure of Process. Conceptual teachers have a leg up on the new AP courses since they're already teaching in a way that emphasizes these elements.

Some courses, such as AP English Literature and Composition and AP Statistics, have yet to be redesigned in this manner and thus do not have specific concept outlines published by the College Board. This is not to say that a conceptual approach is inappropriate for these courses but rather that the teacher must develop concepts and generalizations to guide the course.

Concepts and the Every Student Succeeds Act (ESSA)

In December 2015, President Obama signed a new law that governs education in the United States, replacing the widely unpopular No Child Left Behind (NCLB) law signed by President Bush. The most notable element of this law is that it repeals many powers that NCLB granted to the federal government and returns most of the education-related authority to state and local governments. This shift makes conceptual learning more attainable, as states have more flexibility in accountability constructs. As explained by Rick Hess (2013), "This means that a lot more is possible than used to be the case. It's time to reset expectations. . . . If someone gives you the stock 'must' or 'can't' line, it's worth asking where it says that and whether they're sure that things haven't changed under the new law."

States are still required to test students in literacy and mathematics every year from third to eighth grades, once in ninth through twelfth grade, and in science in high school. But states can determine the format of that assessment. This has allowed several states to pilot innovative assessments. New Hampshire is the first to officially pilot performance assessments in place of standardized tests.

In a press release (2015), New Hampshire Governor Hassan's office explained:

> Performance assessments are complex, multi-part tasks that ask students to apply what they have learned in sophisticated ways. For example, in English, middle school students might submit research papers showing that they know how to analyze and present information from many sources. In math, fourth-graders might design and cost out a new park and write a letter to their board of selectmen arguing their perspective based on their calculations and other evidence.

This shift is great for Concept-Based efforts and great for kids! Conceptual curriculum is a linchpin for authentic transfer to complex tasks. Schools that do this work well should see amazing results on both standardized tests and performance assessments.

Another important part of ESSA is the use of Universal Design for Learning principles (UDL). Somewhat similar to the principle of differentiation, UDL calls for a variety of strategies for presenting information and allowing students to process and demonstrate their learning in unique ways. As this is more of an instructional than curricular strategy, it can easily be paired with Concept-Based Curriculum.

A third part of the new law is an emphasis on literacy, especially for English language learners. Schools will be measured on students' growth in English proficiency as part of their accountability to the state government. Using the Structure of Process to design English proficiency goals will greatly enhance a school's literacy initiatives as will deepening students' contextual understanding through conceptual learning.

Finally, ESSA will provide a few federal grants for schools that innovate. This may be a good avenue for schools or states to pursue as they implement Concept-Based Curriculum and Instruction. This is one to watch if your school would like additional funds for this important work.

Conclusion

We could go on and on discussing different education initiatives and their connection to conceptual learning. We hope, though, that these brief overviews are helpful in building a framework for interpreting new initiatives and integrating these initiatives into your Concept-Based classroom. Without a framework for organizing initiatives, it's very easy for your practice to be overwhelmed with new fads and mandates. Fads will come and go, but a conceptual approach is a powerful foundation that has enough research to support it no matter what other priorities may arise.

Chapter Review

- Using the categories of curriculum, instruction, and assessment, how would you classify the initiatives in your school or district?
- Which connection discussed in this chapter was most surprising for you?
- Which connection discussed in this chapter resonated most with your own experience?
- Choose an education initiative from your school or district that we didn't discuss in this chapter. What connections do you see between that initiative and Concept-Based Curriculum and Instruction?

Conclusion: Imagine What School Could Be . . .

The introduction to this book explains the need for Concept-Based Curriculum and Instruction in the era of innovation. But we require a particular type of innovation, the kind that makes the world a better place. This generation of young people needs to solve problems with a level of complexity and magnitude rarely seen over the course of human history.

Pollution and contamination of the environment, lack of access to resources for a growing number of people, changing weather patterns and ecosystems, the rise and spread of international terrorism, a polarized populace, global poverty, rapid urbanization and large-scale migration—the question for our generation of teachers is, "How do we prepare young people to tackle problems we currently don't know how to solve?"

> The question for our generation of teachers is, "How do we prepare young people to tackle problems we currently don't know how to solve?"

Consider these facts from *The Necessary Revolution* (Senge, 2010):

- More than a third of the world's forests have disappeared in the past 50 years.
- Many diseases are far more prevalent due to toxins in products like food and children's toys.
- Five hundred million chronically underemployed people live in slums, a figure that is increasing by 50 million each year.

And these from *Creating Innovators* (Wagner, 2012):

- Senior business executives say "the greatest innovations of the 21st century will be those that help to address human needs more than those that create the most profit" (p. 6).
- Young people are deeply worried about the future of the planet and want to make a difference more than they want to make money.

Now, put those facts next to these (National Center for Education Statistics, 2016a, 2016b):

- Thirty percent of U.S. students drop out of high school.
- Fifty-four percent of students who start college do not complete it.

Meanwhile,

- The most popular word students selected to describe how they usually feel in school was "bored" (Lyons, 2004).

Businesses want creativity and ideas that address human needs. Today's young people want to do something meaningful, now. Meanwhile, students are bored and opting out of school in droves.

> Picture a school organized around real-world problems that require the flexible application of each subject's concepts with an eye toward identifying and developing students' passions.

More than ever, students need to transfer their learning to real-world, highly dissimilar situations. What we know about dissimilar transfer is that it requires an abstraction to the conceptual level, deeply grounded in a knowledge base. Concept-Based Curriculum and Instruction are major components in how we do it. We can and should start with low-road, academic transfer of learning but quickly move across the spectrum toward high-road, real-world transfer of learning.

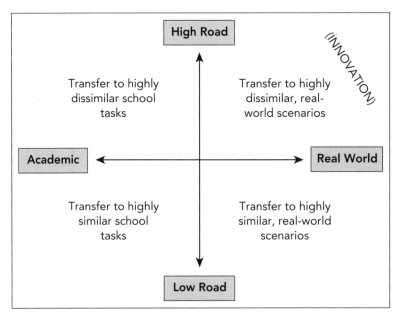

© 2016 Education to Save the World

What would schools look like if we were developing students as collaborative innovators ready to tackle the world's most complex challenges? Picture a school organized around real-world problems that require the flexible application of each subject's concepts with an eye toward identifying and developing students' passions. Students would engage in a variety of experiences that ask them to contribute to building a healthy, sustainable, and just world.

The students in this world-changing school are probably not sitting in desks in rows learning in 50-minute blocks of time, are they? Imagine students choosing an environmental or health situation to solve while they explore concepts of science and mathematics—for example, discovering renewable energy solutions for a major company or reducing infant mortality in a developing nation.

Picture a senior who has identified politics and conflict resolution as his passion. He has chosen to analyze a nation with civil strife, the Central African Republic, and make recommendations for improving the situation. Monday morning starts off with a Skype conference call with a nongovernmental organization from Mozambique that will share lessons learned from the end of that country's civil war in 1992.

After he finishes the call, the student and his team note down action steps and divide the tasks based on each member's interests and expertise. They have two weeks until the next call and before then have two scheduled team meetings and a full-day lab session to work on this project with an expert and the teacher who is mentoring the group. This project is called the Grand Challenge.

At the end of year, the student's team will present its work to a group of experts who will evaluate the students' technical skills, application of conceptual understanding, ability to think critically, and collaboration skills. If the work measures up to the standards for a particular area, they'll receive a badge denoting their skills.

This student has been deepening his understanding of concepts such as authority, rule of law, justice, conflict, and freedom since elementary school. He became a peer counselor in the second grade and has always had a passion for building empathy between disagreeing people or groups. He has read *The Future of Freedom* by Fareed Zakaria, two books on America's democracy by Akhil Amar, and many books on Africa and developing nations. He spent last summer as a peer counselor with youth in a special juvenile detention center where he deepened his skills and understanding of conflict resolution. He has already transferred his understanding of civil strife to several situations, as he analyzed Reconstruction after the U.S. Civil War in eighth grade and Europe after World War II in tenth grade. He feels prepared for the Grand Challenge, as all of his learning experiences have led him to this level of thinking and application.

In addition to the Grand Challenge project and individualized course, he also participates in five courses that all seniors take: *Thinking Like a Mathematician, Thinking Like a Historian, Thinking Like an Engineer, Thinking Like a Journalist,* and *Collaboration*

& Problem Solving. For each of these courses, teachers design learning experiences that help him hone his disciplinary thinking, deepen his conceptual understanding of the discipline, and learn key factual information. Each week he applies what he is learning in one of these courses to real-world problems that his peers have chosen as their Grand Challenge. During these disciplinary thinking labs, a team presents a problem they are facing as part of their Grand Challenge to the students in the class. The students are charged with using the conceptual understanding and thinking of the discipline to help the team better understand the issues, test a possible idea, or develop a solution. Teachers act as coaches who help structure the learning and provide feedback during these labs.

The last element of this student's weekly schedule is coaching a disciplinary thinking lab for sixth graders. This helps him strengthen his thinking in an area of his choice, create community in the school, and give the adult teachers more time to plan rich learning experiences for students and provide effective feedback.

As he thinks about what lies ahead for the week after his Monday morning call, he is excited. He knows the work he is doing is tapping into his passions and purpose. It is also intellectually challenging—he is always uncovering and applying conceptual understanding, evaluating his own thinking using intellectual standards, and applying that thinking to the real world. He believes that his efforts in school will truly change the world—and the great thing is that they will.

The ideas presented in this book, we hope, provide a foundation for moving toward this type of learning. As you try out the strategies and become an expert conceptual teacher, know that you are taking a giant step toward preparing students to tackle problems that we don't yet know how to solve. Your impact can be tremendous—and it's just what the world needs now.

References

A working definition of personalized learning. (2014). Retrieved from https://assets
.documentcloud.org/documents/1311874/personalized-learning-working-definition-
fall2014.pdf

Amabile, T. (1998). How to kill creativity. *Harvard Business Review, 76*(5), 76–87.

Anderson, L. W., & Krathwohl, D. R. (2001). *A taxonomy for learning, teaching, and assessing: A
revision of Bloom's taxonomy of educational objectives.* New York, NY: Longman.

Berger, R. (2003). *An ethic of excellence: Building a culture of craftsmanship with students.*
Portsmouth, NH: Heinemann.

Bransford, J. (2000). *How people learn: Brain, mind, experience, and school.* Washington, DC: The
National Academies Press.

Brookhart, S. M. (2008). *How to give effective feedback to your students.* Alexandria, VA: ASCD.

Brookhart, S. M. (2010). *How to assess higher-order thinking skills in your classroom.* Alexandria,
VA: ASCD.

Bruner, J. S. (1977). *The process of education* (2nd ed.). Cambridge, MA: Harvard University
Press.

Coleman, D. (2011, April 28). Bringing the Common Core to life. Retrieved from http://
usny.nysed.gov/rttt/docs/bringingthecommoncoretolife/fulltranscript.pdf

College Board. (2012). AP: Course & exam redesign. Retrieved from https://secure-media
.collegeboard.org/digitalServices/pdf/ap/AP_CE_Redesign_Brochure_for_Higher_
Ed.pdf

College Board. (2014). AP chemistry: Course and exam description. Retrieved from https://
secure-media.collegeboard.org/digitalServices/pdf/ap/ap-chemistry-course-and-exam-
description.pdf

College Board. (2015a). AP biology: Course and exam description. Retrieved from https://
secure-media.collegeboard.org/digitalServices/pdf/ap/ap-biology-course-and-exam-
description.pdf

College Board. (2015b). AP European history: Course and exam description. Retrieved from
https://secure-media.collegeboard.org/digitalServices/pdf/ap/ap-european-history-
course-and-exam-description.pdf

College Board. (2015c). AP United States history: Course and exam description. Retrieved
from https://secure-media.collegeboard.org/digitalServices/pdf/ap/ap-us-history-course-
and-exam-description.pdf

College Board. (2016a). AP calculus AB and AP calculus BC: Course and exam description. Retrieved from https://secure-media.collegeboard.org/digitalServices/pdf/ap/
ap-calculus-ab-and-bc-course-and-exam-description.pdf

College Board. (2016b). Math test. Retrieved from https://collegereadiness.collegeboard
.org/sat/inside-the-test/math

Donovan, S., & Bransford, J. (2005). *How students learn: History, mathematics, and science in the classroom.* Washington, DC: The National Academies Press. http://dx.doi.org/10.17226/10126

Dweck, C. S. (2007). *Mindset: The new psychology of success.* New York, NY: Random House.

Eiland, D. A. (2008). *Considering race and gender in the classroom: The role of teacher perceptions in referral for special education* (Doctoral dissertation, Michigan State University). Retrieved from https://books.google.com.co/books?id=Z6-b6gSq6lsC&printsec=frontcover&source=gbs_ge_summary_r&cad=0#v=onepage&q&f=false

Erickson, H. L. (2008). *Stirring the head, heart, and soul: Redefining curriculum, instruction, and concept-based learning* (3rd ed.). Thousand Oaks, CA: Corwin.

Erickson, H. L. (2012). Concept-based teaching and learning. Retrieved from http://www.ibmidatlantic.org/Concept_Based_Teaching_Learning.pdf

Erickson, H. L., & Lanning, L. A. (2014). *Transitioning to concept-based curriculum and instruction: How to bring content and process together.* Thousand Oaks, CA: Corwin.

Erickson, H. L., Lanning, L. A., & French, R. (2017). *Concept-based curriculum and instruction for the thinking classroom* (2nd ed.). Thousand Oaks, CA: Corwin.

Fisher, D., Frey, N., & Hattie, J. (2016). *Visible learning for literacy, grades K-12: Implementing the practices that work best to accelerate student learning.* Thousand Oaks, CA: Corwin.

Gardner, H. (2007). *Five minds for the future.* Boston, MA: Harvard Business School Press.

Hamre, B., & Pianta, R. (2006). Student-teacher relationships. *National Association of School Psychologists.* Retrieved from http://www.pearweb.org/conferences/sixth/pdfs/NAS-CBIII-05-1001-005-hamre%20&%20Pianta%20proof.pdf

Hattie, J. (2012). *Visible learning for teachers: Maximizing impact on learning.* London, UK: Routledge.

Hess, R. (2013, March). What ESSA means for teachers and leaders. Retrieved from http://blogs.edweek.org/edweek/rick_hess_straight_up/2016/03/what_essa_means_for_teachers_school_and_system_leaders.html

Lanning, L. A. (2009). *4 powerful strategies for struggling readers, grades 3-8: Small group instruction that improves comprehension.* Thousand Oaks, CA: Corwin.

Lanning, L. A. (2013). *Designing a concept-based curriculum for English language arts: Meeting the common core with intellectual integrity, K-12.* Thousand Oaks, CA: Corwin.

Lyons, L. (2004, June). Most teens associate school with boredom, fatigue [Survey report]. Retrieved from http://www.gallup.com/poll/11893/most-teens-associate-school-boredom-fatigue.aspx

Marzano, R. J. (2007). *The art and science of teaching: A comprehensive framework for effective instruction.* Alexandria, VA: ASCD.

Mehta, J., & Fine, S. (2015). *The why, what, where, and how of deeper learning in American secondary schools.* Students at the Center: Deeper Learning Research Series. Boston, MA: Jobs for the Future.

National Center for Education Statistics. (2016a). *What are the graduation rates for students obtaining a bachelor's degree?* Retrieved from https://nces.ed.gov/fastfacts/display.asp?id=40

National Center for Education Statistics. (2016b). *What are the dropout rates of high school students?* Retrieved from https://nces.ed.gov/fastfacts/display.asp?id=16

National Governors Association Center for Best Practices, & Council of Chief State School Officers. (2010). *Common Core State Standards.* Washington, DC: Authors.

Newmann, F. M., Bryk, A. S., & Nagaoka, J. K. (2001). *Authentic intellectual work and standardized tests: Conflict or coexistence?* Chicago, IL: Consortium on Chicago School Research.

NGSS Lead States. (2013). *Next generation science standards: For states, by states.* Washington, DC: The National Academies Press.

Paul, R. (n.d.). The art of redesigning instruction. Retrieved from http://www.criticalthinking .org/pages/the-art-of-redesigning-instruction/520

Paul, R., & Elder, L. (2008). *The miniature guide to critical thinking concepts and tools.* Dillon Beach, CA: Foundation for Critical Thinking.

Paul, R., & Elder, L. (2013). *How to write a paragraph: The art of substantive writing* (3rd ed.). Tomales, CA: Foundation for Critical Thinking.

Perkins, D. N., & Salomon, G. (1988). Teaching for transfer. *Educational Leadership, 22–32.* Retrieved from http://www.ascd.org/ASCD/pdf/journals/ed_lead/el_198809_perkins .pdf

Press release. (2015, March). Retrieved from http://governor.nh.gov/media/news/2015/ pr-2015-03-05-pace.htm

Producercunningham. (Artist). (2014). *A comparison of the Aral Sea in 1989 (left) and 2014 (right).* Image by NASA. Retrieved from https://en.wikipedia.org/wiki/Aral_Sea#/ media/File:AralSea1989_2014.jpg

Ritchhart, R., Church, M., & Morrison, K. (2011). *Making thinking visible: How to promote engagement, understanding, and independence for all learners.* San Francisco, CA: Jossey-Bass.

Rosenthal, R., & Jacobson, L. (2003). *Pygmalion in the classroom: Teacher expectation and pupil's intellectual development.* Carmarthen, UK: Crown House.

Senge, P. M. (2010). *The necessary revolution: How individuals and organizations are working together to create a sustainable world.* New York, NY: Doubleday.

Spiegel, A. (2012, September). Teachers' expectations can influence how students perform. Retrieved from http://www.npr.org/sections/health-shots/2012/09/18/161159263/ teachers-expectations-can-influence-how-students-perform

Steele, C. (2011). *Whistling Vivaldi: And other clues to how stereotypes affect us.* New York, NY: W. W. Norton.

The college, career, and civic life (C3) framework for social studies state standards: Guidance for enhancing the rigor of K-12 civics, economics, geography, and history. (2013). Silver Spring, MD: National Council for the Social Studies (NCSS).

Tovani, C. (2011). *So what do they really know? Assessment that informs teaching and learning.* Portland, ME: Stenhouse.

Wagner, T. (2012). *Creating innovators: The making of young people who will change the world.* New York, NY: Scribner.

Wathall, J. (2016). *Concept-based mathematics: Teaching for deep understanding in secondary classrooms.* Thousand Oaks, CA: Corwin.

What is project based learning (PBL)? (n.d.). Buck Institute for Education. Retrieved from http://bie.org/about/what_pbl

Why equity? (n.d.). National Equity Project. Retrieved from http://nationalequityproject .org/about/equity

Wiggins, G. P., & McTighe, J. (2005). *Understanding by design* (2nd ed.). Alexandria, VA: ASCD.

Index

Note: In page references, f indicates figures.

example of, 99f
factual knowledge and, 101, 103
summative assessments and, 99–100
See also Assessments
Foundation for Critical Thinking, 30, 36, 55–56
Four corners activity, 49–50
Freedom:
curriculum documents and, 13
different views of, 13, 15
motivation for learning and, 4–5
or equality, 50–51
Frey, N., 2
Future of Freedom, The, 155

G
Gallery walk activity, 51–52, 99f
Geography classroom, 20f, 72, 79
Geometry, 125–126, 125f
Goal-setting:
clarity of, 125–127
classroom culture and, 33
concept-based curriculum and, 15–17
concept-based teaching and, 47–48
conceptual learning and, 62
conceptual relationships and, 115
cooperative learning and, 140
example of, 115f
feedback and, 113, 115, 117
instruction and, 15–17
iterative learning and, 62
learning and, 33–34, 57
motivation and, 113, 115
rubrics and, 115, 117
students and, 113, 115
student self-assessment and, 113, 115
Gold Standard Project-Based Learning, 77, 78f
Grading, 101
portfolio system for, 116–117, 117f
summative assessments and, 100–101
Grand Challenge project, 155–156
Grants, 151
GRASPS model, 77, 79–80
Growth mindset, 31f

H
Harvard Business Review, 1
Hattie, J., 2, 16–17
Health unit, 40f, 41f
Hess, R., 150
High-road transfer, 17, 18f, 103, 104f, 154
See also Transfer
How Students Learn, 47–48, 56
Hurston, Z. N., 105f
Hypotheses lesson framework, 68–73, 69–71f

I
Ideas:
conceptual language and, 38
conceptual learning and, 35–36, 40
intellectual journals and, 31–32
partner coaching and, 32
refining/increasing the sophistication of students', 61
simple/static, 45f
sophisticated/dynamic, 45f
strong, 33
thinking-centered classrooms and, 30
traditional learning and, 35
understanding, 43
Identity, 57
Individuality, students', 34
Individual journaling
See also Journaling
Inequity, educational, 119
Innovation, 1
knowledge and, 2
motivation and, 4
transfer and, 17
Inquiry-based, inductive teaching, 59
Inquiry stations strategy, 140
Instruction:
assessments and, 100
concept-based curriculum and, 6
ultimate goal of, 15–17
Instructional calendar, 85, 89
Instructional tools, 67–68
Intellectual journals, 31–32
Intelligence, 31
International Baccalaureate (IB), 146–147
IQ test, 122
Iterative learning, 40–45, 47
linear learning and, 41–43, 42f
process/goal of, 62
See also Learning

J
Journaling:
cooperative learning and, 140
individual, 48–49
intellectual, 31–32
pre-instructional understandings and, 52
silent, 51

K
Knowledge, 1–2
assessments and, 96–97
balancing breadth of, 149
dimensions, 11f
factual, 11–12
formative assessments and, 101
new, 68

organized systems of, 137
organizing conceptual, 2
prior, 61, 62
procedural, 18
processes and, 18–19
project-based learning and, 77
standards and, 143
structure of, 12–15, 12f, 37, 149
synergistic thinking and, 5
thinking-centered classrooms and, 30
transfer and, 73
understanding and, 10–12
See also Factual knowledge
Krathwohl, D. R., 11, 18

L
Language arts. *See* English language arts
Lanning, L. A., 3, 4, 17–18, 19, 96, 138–139
Leadership:
  motivation for learning and, 4–5
  standards and, 142
Learning, 85, 86–88f
  achieving deeper, 61
  assessments and, 100, 118
  basic truth about, 47–48
  benchmarks for student, 143
  "checklist," 41
  concept-based curriculum and, 5, 6
  concept-based curriculum/instruction
    and, 78f
  conceptual, 29, 34–37, 56, 120f, 121
  cooperative, 139–140
  depth of, 30, 60
  difficulties, 127–128
  environments, 30, 85
  goals for, 33–34, 57
  growth mindset and, 31
  levels of, 17f
  love of, 9
  lower levels of, 21
  metaphors for, 34–35, 35f, 36
  motivation for, 4, 5
  pathways, 85
  personalized, 5, 83–85
  prior, 61
  project-based, 77–83, 78f, 80–82f
  repetitive, 42–43, 92
  rote, 27
  student's control over, 113
  surface, 17f, 62–64
  surface/deep, 62–64, 62f
  that serves students best, 149
  traditional, 34–37, 37f, 40
  transfer of, 15–16
  as uncovering, 58–59
  visual arts, 120f

See also Conceptual learning; Deep learning;
    Iterative learning; Linear learning
Lesson planning:
  conceptual relationships and, 121
  experimenting with, 93
  planners, 85
  workshop model, 73–74
Lessons:
  concept attainment, 53–55, 92
  designing, 67–68
  generating/testing hypotheses and, 69–71f
  mini lessons and, 74
Liberal arts, 4
Linear learning, 40–45
  iterative learning and, 41–43, 42f
  uncover/transfer and, 59
See also Learning
Literacy:
  developing skills and, 55
  media, 4
  standards for, 142–143
  testing and, 150–151
  testing students for, 150–151
  visible learning for, 104f
Low-road transfer, 17, 104f, 154
Lyons, L., 154

M
Macro concepts, 13
Making Thinking Visible, 33
Marzano, R., 68
Mathematics:
  course on, 155
  lesson design structure used in, 74
  repetition and, 92
  testing and, 150
  workshop model and, 73–74
McTighe, J., 79, 138
Meaning:
  assessments and, 96
  concept-based curriculum and, 120
  project-based learning and, 77
  traditional learning and, 35
Memorization:
  comprehension and, 9
  concept attainment and, 54
  concept-based teaching and, 58
  concepts and, 53
  conceptual learning and, 16
  knowledge and, 2
  meaning and, 120
  need for, 92
  traditional learning and, 35, 36
Metaphors, 55, 89, 92
  for learning, 34–35
  understanding of, 49